GO BEYOND

Passion

DISCOVER YOUR DREAM JOB

Julie,
I love your ambition & inspiration!

CHRISTOPHER JAMES LAWRENCE

BALBOA
PRESS

A DIVISION OF HAY HOUSE

Balboa Press books may be ordered through booksellers or by contacting:

Balboa Press
A Division of Hay House
1663 Liberty Drive
Bloomington, IN 47403
www.balboapress.com
1 (877) 407-4847

Because of the dynamic nature of the Internet, any web addresses or
links contained in this book may have changed since publication and may
no longer be valid. The views expressed in this work are solely those
of the author and do not necessarily reflect the views of the publisher,
and the publisher hereby disclaims any responsibility for them.

The author of this book does not dispense medical advice or prescribe the
use of any technique as a form of treatment for physical, emotional, or medical
problems without the advice of a physician, either directly or indirectly. The
intent of the author is only to offer information of a general nature to help you
in your quest for emotional and spiritual well-being. In the event you use any
of the information in this book for yourself, which is your constitutional right,
the author and the publisher assume no responsibility for your actions.

Any people depicted in stock imagery provided by Thinkstock are models,
and such images are being used for illustrative purposes only.
Certain stock imagery © Thinkstock.

Print information available on the last page.

ISBN: 978-1-5043-5007-5 (sc)
ISBN: 978-1-5043-5009-9 (hc)
ISBN: 978-1-5043-5008-2 (e)

Library of Congress Control Number: 2016901981

Balboa Press rev. date: 3/16/2016

It took a village...

*My grandparents, all of you, the matriarchs and patriarchs
that provide my wisdom and yearning to work hard*

*My parents, David and Yvonne, the ceaseless childlike
wonder and laughter in my heart, my tenacity to survive*

*My step-parents, Darrell and Sandy, the voices
of reason that remain, still, my conscience*

*My siblings, Shayne and Jamie, the bravery
in my soul and my reason*

My step-siblings, all of you, the diversity that keeps me open

*My aunts, uncles, and cousins, the opportunity
and challenge are my carriage and fire*

My partner, Vince, the steady ground on which I walk

*My mentor, Kyle, the sounding board for every single
consideration, my permission to fail and succeed*

My friends, Melanie, Sara, and Stephanie, the kindness in my spirit

*My pride and joy, Hiro, my dog, the master of
space and time, my master of happiness*

Without all of you my life would not be bearable, possible or joyful.

This is all for you, with love.

CONTENTS

INTRODUCTION

THE STRUGGLE IS REAL!

What is fulfillment? Denis E. Waitley, an American motivational speaker and best-selling author, said, "It is not in the pursuit of happiness that we find fulfillment, it is in the happiness of pursuit." Waitley is telling us what we have heard so many times before—it's about the journey, not the destination. There is truth in what he says and it comes with challenges when we consider our careers.

I graduated from college in 2004 with honours, ready to take on the world. I had targeted the company I wanted to work for: WestJet, the fun, friendly, and highly successful airline. This was my own destination but unlike Waitley's statement I didn't enjoy the journey in getting to the destination. I had applied, on seven separate occassions, to positions in WestJet over a course of six months. Admittedly, now, it doesn't seem like a long time but I was ambitious and wanted to get started right away. I interviewed and was told "no" on three separate occasions. Eventually, on my fourth attempt, I landed a position as an administrator in their flight attendant training department. I thought, *This is it! My dream job!* I had arrived at my destination.

At the time, WestJet received over 4000 résumés a month. They were the pinnacle of an inclusive and positive corporate culture in Canada and they had amazing benefits. It was an honour to be selected to work for them, and yet, after just a few short months, I found myself relentlessly dissatisfied with the status quo. My job wasn't what I thought it would be. I received accolades and acknowledgement for my work efforts and that kept me going for a while but I wasn't happy to do the work I had been assigned. I thought I could fix the problem with more education. I assumed more education would open more doors and somehow create more satisfaction, so I was constantly taking classes and certifications. I was still feeling inadequate, so I thought I needed more money, a better title, and more responsibility. I got those too. None of it helped so I blamed the company and my boss. After a few years, I left WestJet feeling bitter and unhappy, heading for the oil and gas industry where I could make my way as a Business Analyst. But this cycle followed me and repeated itself over and over again until I was clinically depressed, thirty pounds overweight, and really unhappy.

After just over 10 years in corporate Calgary I was ready to leave, not because corporate Calgary was the problem, but because I was sick and tired of trying so hard to find fulfillment. I was a free agent and only had a small inkling of what I wanted to do. I knew I wanted to work for myself and I knew I wanted to help people—It is because of this journey that I found myself in the realm of career and life coaching and am finally experiencing career fulfillment.

Confucius said, "Choose a job you love, and you will never have to work a day in your life". There are many well-meaning, inspiring catch phrases like this yet they are misleading and provide little to no direction. I can say that as a Career and Life Coach, I am in a job that I love absolutely and yet I can absolutely say I do have to work and sometimes it is hard work, probably harder than I have ever worked in my entire life. Having your dream job is not always an easy walk in the park. It can be a long and difficult path but one that comes with the reward of wanting to wake up in the morning and being fulfilled by making a meaningful contribution to your work. So how do you discover what meaningful career you were mean to have?

Choosing a career has never been more difficult. This point can be illustrated using a simple example involving menu choices at two different restaurants. Envision, for a moment, walking into a high-class restaurant. It's modern and chic. There is a big lobby, one massive modern chandelier that reminds you of fire and ice, and the tables are pristine with silver and glass. The server introduces herself in the most professional of ways and hands you the menu. The one-page menu is broken into three sections, narrow and simple:

Appetizers	*Mains*	*Desserts*
Creamy Sundried Tomato Soup	Steak. 10oz	Crème Brûlée
Deconstructed Chef Salad	Slow Roasted Chicken	Chocolate Mousse
	Pork Tenderloin	
	Duck Confit	
	Vegetable Lasagna	

Make your selections. What will you eat?

Now, envision for a moment walking into a run-of-the-mill all-day breakfast joint. It is also modern but the place is crowded. The friendly server crouches down to introduce himself, jokes with you for a moment, and hands you a menu. The menu is three or four pages long and has a number of sections. The first page looks like this:

Breakfast

Fresh Squeezed Juices & Fruit
- Fresh Squeezed Orange Juice

Fruit Bowl
- Scrumptious assortment of fresh fruits, with nuts and raisins

Cereals & Breads
- Bread Basket
- Assortment of fresh baked fruit breads and muffins

- Honey Almond Granola with Fruit
- Natural cereal of honey toasted oats, raisins, almonds and dates
- Fruit Breads; English Muffin; Muffins; Bagel
- Vegan, Organic Fruit & Nut Granola

Pancakes
- Buttermilk Pancakes
- Blueberry Pancakes
- Original Oatmeal Pancakes

French Toast

Specialty Drinks

Mimosa - fresh squeezed orange juice and champagne

Bellini Cocktail - peach purée and Prosecco sparkling wine

Cranberry Fizz - Prosecco sparkling wine and cranberry juice

Peach Tea Cooler - Vodka, peach puree, and fresh brewed ice tea

Lunch Menu

Soup, Salads & Starters
- Bayberry Wings
- Clam Chowder
- Angry Wings

Mains
- Rustic Pizza
- Margherita Pizza
- Seafood Pizza

Salads
- Spinach Salad
- Garden Salad
- Classic Chicken Caesar
- Lobster Salad

Burgers and Sandwiches
- Waldorf Chicken Croissant
- Vegetable Panini
- Turkey Burger
- Oven Roasted Turkey Sandwich
- Lobster Salad Sandwich

Make your selections. What will you eat this time?

I suspect making choices at the first restaurant was much easier for you and took less time than the second restaurant. This is because at the second restaurant you have more selections to choose from. When we have more to choose from it makes it more difficult to make a choice. One-hundred years ago our career choices were limited to our region, education, economic status, and our knowledge of what careers existed. While some of those limitations still exist today, they can be overcome more easily by social programs and technology. In fact, technology has not only created tens of thousands of unique jobs in the last one hundread years, but also allowed us to be aware of their existence. What we end up doing is choosing the same thing over and over again because it's what is comfortable to us. We keep going back to what we know and never changing. Just like in a restaurant. We don't always choose what is new but rather keep eating what we already know. Our menu of careers has grown from possibly hundreds of jobs to millions!

This can make your choice overwhelming. Sometimes this creates what I call the "unknown void". The unknown void is a place inside of us where we can't seem to be satiated and it causes intense feelings of inadequecy and rumination. This is where we feel unable to make a choice and will often use the phrase "I don't know" when asked about our career and life aspirations. If you have ever felt like this, this is the correct book for you!

If you are part of Generation-Y (people born between 1980 to 2000), then you may find this decision even more difficult. As Generation-Y we are often accused of being ungrateful and disloyal because we have been born with more opportunities than any previous generations yet it appears we take it for granted. I would argue that for Generation-Y, it isn't about being deliberately ungrateful or disloyal but rather about being the first generation to have so much choice and convenience that we aren't quite sure how to work hard and focus like the generations that came before us.

One-hundred years ago things were a lot clearer. If you were an average woman, you were likely going to stay at home with your kids. If you were an average man, you were going to do what your father did or you would invest in whatever education you could afford, and that was your job for as long as you could sustain it. The career choices were easy (although easy does not imply pleasant). This was the way it was for thousands of years. Only in the last one-hundred years or so has this changed and it has changed dramatically.

So, yes, we have the incredible gift of many choices; however, when we have too much choice we sometimes don't even know where or how to be loyal or grateful for what we have. Generation-Y, in my opinion, more than any generation previously does not know how to make a decision and stick with it. We have been raised that "we can do anything we want" and "the world is your oyster". Then you add in the convenience of having any answer we require at our fingertips because of technology... well, let's just say that the expectations of ourselves and others are unreasably high. Because of this we continually let ourselves down, we aren't "noticed" as the next social media star.

It isn't just about Generation-Y any longer. This is affecting every generation now alive. I have the same conversations with those under 30 years old that I have with those over 60 years old.

So what can you do? The intention of this book is to take a holistic approach to your career journey, to help you take the little inspirations and put them into practical application so that you can finally discover what career fulfillment is to you. We must look at every area of your life, not just your skills and abilities. Why? Because you are virtually accessible 24 hours a day, 7 days a week. You spend the best part of your day and the best part of your life at work. It's no longer just about your job, it's about your whole life!

Throughout this book you will read about practical tools and real-life examples based on my clients' experiences to help guide you in discovering what your dream job should be. For privacy reasons, you should know that no names in this book are real and that enough of the details of their stories have been changed to ensure they can not be identified.

Why This Book & The Problem With Self-Help

There are so many self-help books, movies, and talks out there. Everyone is a coach or a motivational speaker or an author. I really struggled with the idea of writing this book because there is so much out there already. In my opinion some of what is out there is less than helpful and, in some cases, very damaging. There is a new regime of people coming out of the woodwork that virtually boycott the entire self-help industry. I can understand why. Everyone has a checklist, process, system or promise that will produce some magical result. They tout why the other systems don't work and why theirs is the best system. Let's explore these so that you can see the pitfalls people fall into and how you should approach this book.

The self-help market can reinforce feelings of inadequacy. This causes us to spend more money and time but in the end we tend to accomplish less. After trying a few programs many feel that they have an unsolvable problem and keep investing more and more and more to try and resolve it. This leads to the second problem...

Self-help can be another form of avoidance. I see this with my clients. They invest in a program and will come in to talk about their problems and have a breakthrough. This is awesome! Sometimes that is the goal! The challenge here is that they become addicted to the breakthrough, the "solving" portion of the coaching and therefore take little or no action to actually make the work long lasting or sustainable. I see this a lot in the coaching industry itself. Personally, I pride myself on my dedication to ongoing learning; however, I too have fallen into the trap of buying a program with the hope of some miracle. At the end of the day, no matter what program you choose to invest in, no matter what book you choose to read, no matter what speaker you follow religiously. *Nothing happens without you taking action and doing the work!*

Self-help programs can create unrealistic expectations. Self-help marketers often give you the impression that their program is the only program that works or they say this is the only system you will ever need. Some even say, "I was the first so this is the real system—it works". With this type of program, you get "follow these steps and don't veer from them at all and then watch what happens".

Inevitably, what can happen is that we buy a program, it doesn't work for one of the three reasons listed above and then we are so tarnished by the experience that we think what we want isn't achievable or we buy the next best program and start to speak negatively about what didn't work about the last one we invested in. This puts us in a state of perpetual rationalization. We spend more time planning and organizing our change than actually doing the work to change. As Russian writer Leo Tolstoy reminds us, "Everyone thinks of changing the world, but no one thinks of changing himself."[1] Change requires action and actual hands-on work.

> *"Everyone thinks of changing the world,*
> *but no one thinks of changing himself."*
> - Leo Tolstoy

If this is the first self-help book you have ever picked up... congratulations! I hope you enjoy it!

Whether this is your first or your one-hundredth self-help book, I encourage you to observe how you approach this material and ask yourself if the way you are approaching it is going to yield the results you desire.

This is not magic and it won't happen without your effort. We are in a society that everything you could possibly ever want to know is right at your fingertips. Literally! This is why I am asking you to be present to the work that you desperately want to do (especially if this isn't the first self-help book you have ever read). Stop investing in more programs, more training, more books, more time at conferences listening to speakers, and more, more, more until you have actually picked one direction and seen it through to the end. In fact, stop listening to what others have to say for a while (as long as your personal safety or the safety of other humans or animals is not in direct danger). You need to hear your own voice, and that's exactly what this book will do for you. Maybe you will hear it for the first time in your life! Once you have done that then you can consider what it looks like to engage in more programs to keep you sharp.

The good news is that any of the programs on the market have the possibility to work for you if followed correctly. You have chosen this book as one of your approaches and I am confident that once you get to the end, if you do the work presented, you will feel confident about the choices you make and seeing the results you want to achieve.

---

[1] Leo Tolstoy quote. (n.d.). Retrieved November 15, 2015, from http://www.brainyquote.com/quotes/quotes/l/leotolstoy105644.html

You may notice throughout this book that I, too, occasionally leverage the above listed self-help tactics for my programs and material. Why? For the same reason that other self-help marketers do this... it's good for business! But I don't want to be part of the problem. I want to be seen as part of the solution. I am in this field because I LOVE what I do for a living. I love my career and I desperately want you to as well. That is how I meet my need for contribution. Let me say this now. If you are not ready, willing or able to do the work outlined here, I will happily refund whatever money you have invested in this book so that you can find the program you are truly willing to invest your time and effort into. I want this to be a part of the solution to your career fulfillment, not another book you have on the shelf with good intentions.

CHAPTER 1

IT'S NOT JUST ABOUT YOUR JOB—IT'S ABOUT YOUR LIFE!

It's not just about your job—it's about your life!

Now that we have that out of the way, we can begin our work together.

So many of my coaching clients come to me because they are seeking work-life balance. **Work-life balance refers to a correct prioritization between work and lifestyle.** Essentially, it equates to a separation of what we do to make money and how we spend the rest of our time. We then use dollars earned to invest in things we value. In an obvious way, the diagram below explains the perceived flow:

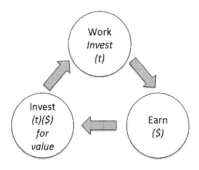

Perceived **Work-Life Balance Model**
(t) = time, ($) = money

At first glance, the model appears to make sense. We work, which is an investment of our time. Ideally, we make decent money for what we do. Then we invest that money in things we believe are important or have value to us. This is what most of the 5-billion working people in the world currently do.[2] The problem with this diagram is that all of the circles are the same size and they don't necessarily meet any of our six human needs: certainty, variety (uncertainty), love and connection, significance, contribution, and growth[3]. In simpler terms, there is no indication of personal fulfillment or dissatisfaction represented in these circles. Truthfully, the diagram looks more like what we see in the ***Actual* Work-Life Balance Model**, on the following page, in North American Culture and increasingly so in other first world nations.

In the ***Actual* Work-Life Balance Model** we can see that we sometimes invest more time at work than we typically feel we are paid to do. This can be because our perception is that we don't make enough money to do the amount or type of work we are required to. This perception is also skewed, particularly if we don't enjoy the type of work we do, because we spend the best part of our day and the prime of our lives doing something that perhaps doesn't put us in a peak state. It can also be skewed as a result of constantly being connected. Even jobs that you used to be able to leave work at work somehow find a way to follow us home.

[2] Evans, Lisa. 'Global Employment: What Is The World Employment Rate?'. *The Guardian*. N.p., 2011. Web. 9 Aug. 2015.
[3] Tony Robbins Blog,. 'The 6 Human Needs: Why We Do What We Do - Tony Robbins Blog'. N.p., 2013. Web. 9 Aug. 2015.

<u>Actual</u> Work-Life Balance Model
(t) = time, ($) = money

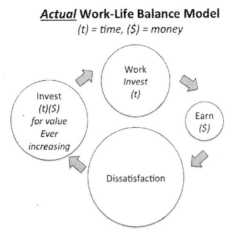

One of my former clients, Janelle, worked for a major retail chain in Calgary. She had a typical swipe-in swipe-out frontline position; however, because of new technology (namely cell phones), she was constantly on call because of staff calling in sick and the necessity to fill in at other stores; she was also required to do work-related reading in her own time; and she had to show up 15 minutes early, unpaid or she would be marked late. It was not unheard of for her boss or co-workers to text her during her down time to change a shift or to ask her to fill in. Our world has changed and so have the expectations of our employers as well as our own expectations.

Still speaking to the Work and Earn circles in the diagram, there are exceptions to this. Some people do feel they are paid enough money, so perhaps their Work and Earn circles would be balanced. But then we come into Dissatisfaction. This circle represents a multitude of unfulfilled desires based on our perception. Our day-to-day tasks, bad co-workers or boss, negative working environment, living pay-cheque-to-pay-cheque, not enough change, and too much change are all examples of what fall into the Dissatisfaction circle.

When we are highly dissatisfied we look for external stimulation. This is why the Invest (t)($) for Value circle is bigger and ever increasing. This is because we are trying to find satisfaction when we can't find any in our jobs. The more we make, the more we spend.

This model would become increasingly complex as we add in things like personal relationships, health and wellness, and personal obligations. I'll spare you another diagram but I hope you will agree that it is obvious that work satisfaction goes far beyond this concept of work-life balance.

I have worked for and with organizations who have invested millions of dollars into work-life balance initiatives. Most of which completely fail! Why is this?

The companies that invest in work-life balance will provide things like flex-time, designated time off days (DTOs), earned days off (EDOs), options to purchase additional vacation time, added benefits plans and packages, stock options, etcetera. The problem is each employee's values system is completely different. So instead of educating leadership to get to the root of a single employee's personal satisfaction, they try to encompass what they believe is value using averages done on surveys and perceived value. Some studies may suggest that what we think we are looking for is not what we actually want. Therefore, it may be reasonable to assume that what we have scored on a survey is merely a band-aid fix. They likely asked the question, "Would you value more time off?" on a scale of 1 to 5, with 5 being highly valued and 1 being not valued at all. If they had asked, "Would you like to know that your boss can help you influence your job to get the most meaningful tasks and make your job worth working for or would you just like more time off?", we might have ended up with a very different result. Personally, I like having extra time off but not at the expense of spending my time at work being miserable. That said, I have worked with many and coached many who don't want the extra time off because they don't know what they would do with it.

We seek work-life balance but not many have found an acceptable definition of the concept. What we do know is that it is not an equal balance in regards to time.

24 hours a day – 8 hours for sleeping – 8 hours for working = 8 hours for me!

But 8 hours for me gets eaten away by getting to and from work, dressing and showering to be presentable at work, making meals to eat at work (or before or after if you buy your lunch), family and relational obligations, and general household and personal care eat up most of the rest of the time. This perspective certainly comes from a lack perspective rather than an abundance perspective.

Life is more fluid than what we might expect work-life balance to be on paper. With that fluidity, we will fall in and out of balance with most of our time being spent out of balance based on a traditional definition. With this comes the "as soon as" phrase, the ritual of getting around to the enjoyment of life "as soon as" I've accomplished the next thing. This is a dissatisfaction trap!

There is no perfect one-size fits all.

Work-life balance does not exist! When clients say, "I need work-life balance", what I hear is "I am unfulfilled in both my job and my personal life. I have no satisfaction in what I do. I don't feel like I am contributing to anything important or meaningful". What I want is for you to be free so you can spend the best part of your life doing something that completely fulfills and inspires you. I say this because when we are fulfilled and inspired it extends the best part of our life and we become the person that inspires others to live their best life.

> *"When we are fulfilled and inspired*
> *it extends the best part of our life*
> *and we become the person*
> *that inspires others to live their best life."*
> - Christopher Lawrence

I have seen my clients struggle with the trap of trying to define work-life balance and then, when they think they have something good on paper, they head to the boss to try to influence and negotiate for more meaningful work or a raise. Even if they are successful in this endeavor, it sometimes doesn't take long to come back to that place of dissatisfaction.

Remember Janelle? She thought that more money would help satisfy her craving for work-life balance. With some coaching and her tenacity to take risks and challenge herself, she successfully negotiated a four-dollar per hour raise in her retail job. Now this doesn't sound like a lot but when you calculate that over the course of a year for a full-time position it is over eight-thousand dollars a year!

A raise this large is almost unheard of in the retail industry and was a huge win for Janelle and a wonderful achievement! But it wasn't long before she was unsatisfied again. It wasn't just about the money, it wasn't just about the job, but it was about her life. When this happened, as it does for so many, Janelle became confused. She began to ruminate and became depressed. This is because she had a belief about money similar to the model shown earlier in the **Perceived Work-Life Balance Model.** No one had taught her (or any of us for that matter) how to hear her own voice and define personal satisfaction.

I would like you to know that I am a Certified Master Coach and have the credentials and professional experience to write this book, but you don't care about that. What you care about is that I have experiences that make this relatable, don't you? You didn't invest your time and money in this book because I have initials behind my name. You invested in this book so you could get your very own outstanding results. The very best way to get results is to look at someone who has done what you are hoping to achieve—in this case, evolving any job into your dream job—and take what they have done to make it work for you in your circumstance.

So far, in my life, I have worked for over 15 companies and have held approximately 23 different job titles. I have made as little as $2.00 an hour and in one company made well over 6-figures a year. In all of these jobs, I started out feeling amazing and motivated and left them feeling mostly dissatisfied and unhappy—and very confused!

I have explored traditional career coaching and counseling. While these people do very good work and certainly hold a place in our society, it isn't my style. My experience with traditional career counseling was as such:

1. Introductory phone call or session
2. Make an investment of time and money
3. Do some personality and skills assessments and have a bit of conversation
4. Get a list of job titles, have a couple of "get-realistic" conversations because writing or art isn't a legitimate way to make a living
5. Pick some vague direction to explore or get "validated" that "you are in the job you should be"

I have seen a few of these clients who weren't completely sullied by their previous career counseling experiences. They have come to me directly, more often than not with desperation and tears, looking for something more or different.

My goal is to get you using any and all of the experiential learning you have had. Experiential learning is learning that comes from living life. This is learning that you have from your own stories and hearing other people's stories. This is learning that comes from not allowing your experiences to stay in silos but rather combining life lessons and learning you have already had to find new ways of thinking about achieving your goals and overcoming obstacles.

Jake, a blue-collar worker was one of these clients. I was the third career professional that he had seen that year. With tears streaming down his face, he told me how he continued to feel unseen and unheard and all of the other help he had received wasn't working. He had been given a list of job titles and a skills assessment that he handed to me tentatively, hands trembling. He had wanted to get out of the blue-collar work and was told that it wasn't realistic for his previous experience but he could look at getting a degree and that might help. But why would he because the money he was making now was so good? He was supporting a small family, so additional expensive education wasn't an option for him at this time. He felt stuck and alone, he wanted off the tools. He was brought up, and it was reinforced by his experiences with parents, friends, and counselors, to believe in five key myths that I think all people who are dissatisfied in their career experience. They are as follows:

Myth 1: You have a calling, everybody does

Similar offenders are:
- I'm looking for that "one" job that will make me happy
- For every person there is one dream job

Reality: Some people are very clear on what they were meant to do for their career and are focused in pursuing their desire. Others might feel like they have a calling, but they have no idea what it is. Some will feel like they don't have a calling–and that's okay too. Also, look at all the jobs in the world, as mentioned there are around 5 billion ways to do a job in the world and counting.[4] How could you possibly have a clear calling with so many options?

Myth 2: You should do what you are good at

A similar offender is:
- "Do something you are passionate about"

Reality: Passion is fleeting and you are probably really good at a lot of things that you never want to be a part of your job. Look at all of the people passionate about politics and religion and yet many of them do not belong in those industries. A dream job can build off your passions and then it should also focus on the day-to-day tasks that fill you up. That's what the job is, isn't it? Not the title, not the money, it's not even what you are passionate about. It is about what you do from one day to the next. People blame the title and money though, don't they? Let's bust that myth too!

Myth 3: Dream jobs pay a lot of money and have a good title

Reality: This depends on whether you are motivated by money or purpose. We have an assessment at Change My Life Coaching that

---

[4] Evans, Lisa. 'Global Employment: What Is The World Employment Rate?'. *the Guardian*. N.p., 2011. Web. 9 Aug. 2015.

can show you if you are authentically motivated by cash. The truth is that most people are not authentically motivated by money. And even when it comes to purpose, as humans, we tend to be best motivated by short-term rewards and quick wins.

As for titles, job titles are misleading. To illustrate my point here are some of the job titles I have come across that can be very misleading:

- Retail Sales Rep
- Customer Service Agent
- Merchandising Assistant
- Photograph Printer
- Movie Rental Representative
- Commercial/Residential Painter
- Reprographics Printer
- Recruiter
- Coordinator
- Business Analyst
- Communications Lead
- Manager
- Life Coach
- Career Counselor
- Project Manager

Those are really a very small sampling. I would love to describe how all of these are misleading but I will take just one to illustrate the point. Let's look at Movie Rental Representative. The client that held this job mostly had cleaning duties, a tiny bit of cash register work, and a lot of cash office work. For interest's sake, they did also rent the occasional movie to customers as well.

To help my clients strip away the title and money I have created a tool called "Going Beyond Your Passion: Discovering Your Job Fit". I have included the steps in Chapter 4 for this tool in this book. One of my clients, Kerrie, a 29-year-old, part-time small business owner who worked as an occupational therapist during the day, had this to say: "Where was this tool earlier in my life? I totally get why I hate what I have been spending my time doing. Now I know what I need to focus on and hire out. You're right, it had nothing to do with the title or money."

Myth 4: There is no such thing as a dream job, everybody has to work hard, get over it!

This is unfortunately where people get stuck the most.

Reality: Dream jobs do exist, but everyone has their own interpretation of what this means. I have tried to define a dream job as follows:

- A dream job is where at least 80% of the day-to-day tasks fill you up.
- Where you want to wake up to do your job no less than 80% of the time.
- Where your need for contribution, connection, significance, certainty, variety, and growth are mostly met and where they can't be, you can easily achieve these in other areas of your life
- Where your values (what is important to you) and your beliefs (how you operate) are in line with what you do to make a living

The challenge, of course, is that this is my definition and this could change over time. It might not be yours. One thing that is certain though, if you believe that there is no such thing as a dream job...you are correct. There isn't and you will never find it. You must believe that it is possible. Perception truly is everything!

Myth 5: I will always be happy in my dream job

Reality: The only constant in our lives is change. Our circumstances, jobs and titles, and financial situations change. The people around us–clients, customers, bosses, co-workers, they all change. The truth is we all have bad days now and again, don't we?

This, by the way, is why when my clients find me to discover their dream job, the first couple of months are the honeymoon phase. We make lots of progress, but then at the three to six month mark we are talking about relationships, money, physical fitness, everything you can imagine, because it is all part of an indivisible whole.

> *"It's not just about your job, it's about your life!"*
> - Christopher Lawrence

This is why, unlike traditional career counseling, this can't be done for most people over night or in three sessions or in five sessions. That is only a starting point. You'll get some great stuff, but it's not enough.

One of my clients said this better than I did. Her name was Carrie. She is 32 years old and works for an airline. She said, "Christopher, you taught me to practice hearing my truest, purest inner voice. You have no idea the impact that this has had on my life. Now when change happens, I already know what I need to do. I don't lose sleep over organizational changes, or changes in my role because I always have a plan. I know what fills me up and makes me feel strong and if that changes, I know how to discover it again. I will always be grateful."

This is what we have to do with you too! We have to get clear on where you want to be and how you are going to get there. You need to hear your own voice and remove the confusion about what is acceptable in your own life.

To do this we are going to work through the Dream Job Evolution Process in this book. See the **Dream Job Evolution Process** diagram below. I am going to build this analogy to driving a car. Let's say, for sake of illustration, that you are a brand new driver with no experience and you decided to get on the freeway at speeds of 110 kilometers per hour during rush hour, things probably aren't going to go very well for you. Perhaps, in the career realm, you have been "driving" for a long time but something still isn't working for you (or you wouldn't be reading this book) then usually the safest and best thing to do is to pull the vehicle over. If life is like a vehicle because it is going from destination to destination, then in this circumstance we must...

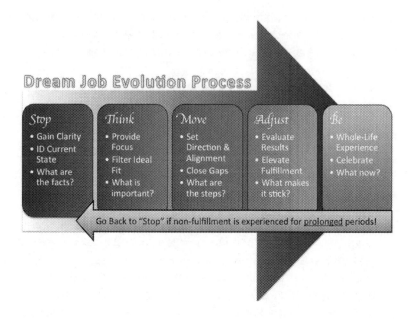

Stop so that we can gain clarity. If we don't stop, then it is like trying to take a picture while you are driving. It's dangerous and unchartered. We are going to bring the vehicle to a stop so that you can take a picture of where you are. We will answer the question *"What are the facts?"*.

Then we must **Think** so that we can provide ourselves with focus. The vehicle still isn't moving at this point but we are getting close to putting that key back in the ignition. This time though, we are going to look at the entire inside and outside of the vehicle to ensure we understand how to operate it. We will answer the question *"What is important?"*.

After we **Think** we will **Move**; very slowly at first. We are going to set the direction in the GPS and make sure that we are aligned. We do this by ensuring we have all of the tools we need and examining if we are actually ready for the road trip we desire. We will answer the question *"What are the next steps?"*.

Once the vehicle is moving we will need to **Adjust** in order to gain speed and build momentum. To do this we will evaluate how we are doing and check in with our personal fulfillment. We will elevate ourselves as we answer the question *"What makes it stick?"*. Here we are speaking specifically to sustaining the vehicle on the chosen road.

Once we are rolling at a good pace and have a nice rhythm we must *Be* with the vehicle. This implies that driving has become part of our unconscious mind. It is natural to us now. This allows us to enjoy the whole experience of driving and we can (and must) take the time to celebrate our successes so that driving the vehicle is always enjoyable. And, just to make sure we don't fall asleep at the wheel, we will answer the question *"What now?"*.

Finally, we will talk about what happens if we *do* happen to fall asleep at the wheel and forget what we are doing or lose sight of our destination. Here we may again need to **Stop**, especially if we are experiencing non-fulfillment for prolonged periods! This is represented by the smaller arrow with the text "Go back to "stop" if non-fulfillment is experienced for prolonged periods!" I say prolonged periods because we will all go through periods of non-fulfillment and discomfort during our working lives. The answer is not always about starting over or jumping ship. The answer is to observe.

You can see in this diagram, no matter where you are on your journey you can move left or right at any time if you need to. The whole process to get you results is wonderfully linear on paper, but at times you may be required to move left or right out of sync. That's real life and that's wonderful, even if we can't see it as a blessing at the time.

What you will experience, by following the process outlined in this book, will get you out of confusion and rumination. It will bust your own belief and values systems that aren't serving you and keeping you exactly where you are. By the end of this, you will feel inspired to work hard and evolve from where you are now into your dream job so that you can have a Whole-Life Experience.[5]

This is work. It will take time and there are no over-night fixes but I guarantee the results are worth it. In fact, I believe in this so much that if you are unsatisfied with this book I will refund the price you paid for this book and you can keep the book for someone who you think it might be a better fit for![6] Like I said, I want to be part of the solution, not part of the problem.

Do you remember Jake and Janelle? In the end, Jake found a way to shift his perception around his job and stayed where he was until he was able to start his own business. It involved doing the same thing, but it became so much more satisfying because he was leading the team and wasn't on the tools any longer. He is an insanely successful businessman today because we were able to get him hearing his own voice. As for Janelle, she transferred with her company to another city so that she could go to fashion school!

While these two stayed in the same industry, I want you to know that, as of writing this book, I have worked with over 100 clients. It is all possible! I have seen clients learn to love making $50,000 a year while supporting a family. I have seen clients pick up and move to the Middle East to discover their dream jobs. I have seen clients open their own businesses and others close their business doors to go back to full-time employment. I have seen clients stay exactly where they are and learn to love their jobs again. I have also seen clients do nothing and experience no change or results (believe it or not this takes more energy and time than changing does). It is all possible!

All you have to do is believe it to be true and I promise you will be successful!

---

[5] A meaningful Whole-Life Experience is about having an experience or series of experiences where we are able to sustain our judgment for a period of time and see the blessing in all of it rather than rushing to any conclusions. What this means is that we have to be grateful and celebrate every aspect of our journey. This is what ultimately locks in those good feelings that make us want to keep growing and trying.
[6] Email info@ChangeMyLifeCoaching.ca to let us know what you thought and if you desire a refund simply attach a proof of purchase.

*"All you have to do is believe it is all possible
and I promise you will be successful!"*
        - Christopher Lawrence

Let's get started RIGHT NOW!

**There is just one more thing. We have provided a workbook
to be used alongside this book. It will help you complete
the activities listed inside.** The workbook has laid out all of
the activities contained in this book in a linear format with
examples and descriptions. You can download this workbook
at www.ChangeMyLifeCoaching.ca/workbook **or you can simply
use a journal of your choosing.**

CHAPTER 2

STOP TO DETERMINE THE FACTS

It seems ironic that you are probably reading this book to get going and at our first step I am asking you to stop. I believe the analogy of driving speaks to the reason why stopping is our very first step. If we are driving too fast while trying to take a picture, the picture ends up blurry. To gain clarity we must pull the vehicle over to look at where we currently are. This does not mean that we stop our journey, but simply that we are going to ensure we enjoy the journey. In order to enjoy the journey, we must take note if our vehicle needs gas or perhaps it needs to be cleaned inside and out. Maybe pieces need to be replaced or repaired.

In a literal sense, what I am asking you to do is to temporarily stop making decisions and stop trying to figure things out just for a little bit of time.

Michael, a client that worked with me for two years would sometimes get stuck in analysis paralysis. He would constantly try to get *Moving* and then *Adjust*. In fact, this is where most of my clients start. They want to get moving right out of the gate. They start to see a lot of initial results, but inevitably end up back in dissatisfaction. Many of them have to have this experience before they are ready to do the real work. I call this the Honeymoon Phase because everything is really exciting when you start to coach and results come quickly then when the vacation is over, the real work begins.

Michael is one of my typical clients. In fact, he might look familiar to you. He and others will often look for the quick fix. These people are relentlessly dissatisfied with the status quo. They often carry the following traits:

- Constantly talking about the problems at work and sometimes blame other people
- Often take different courses, certificates, certifications, and designations because they feel that more education will help them feel more satisfied and move around within a company (which it can, but these people seem to lack a specific and clear direction on where they are going)
- Feel that without a degree, masters, or doctorate that they will not be able to go where they want to go
- Seem relentlessly dissatisfied with the way things are
- Are typically change friendly and often the initiators of change until they realize that the change didn't really solve the problem – which, unbeknownst to them, is actually their own internal struggle and has little or nothing to do with the boss, company, or salary
- Feel that there is no job out there for them and they will never be satisfied with work

What I like about Michael is that he was constantly taking action. It was easy to get Michael motivated to do the work, and by the time he came to me he was ready and willing to do whatever it took to find some answers and a fulfilling direction for his career.

On the flip side we have Donna. Donna worked with me for six months and she did none of the above. She is the Steady Eddy client. She might look a little more familiar to you if Michael didn't resonate. People like this:

- Have an interest in furthering themselves but are too comfortable to do anything about it
- Are comfortable, unmotivated and tend to analyze every possible angle of a situation, thereby not taking any action or taking action so slowly that they miss opportunities
- Use a lot of "Yeah, true. But…" statements

- Are more interested in talking about the problem than solving it
- Typically are not change friendly and tend to resist change because "we've always done it this way"
- Feel stuck, stagnant, unable to move

To be fair, I am stereotyping here and yes I have presented this information in polarities. Our world is made up of binary: black/white, in/out, good/bad. My intent is to show you that any one of these things can work against you. You might have a combination of them or you might be in your own category. For instance, you see the benefits of change, but you want someone else to do it. Perhaps you don't resonate with any of these things and would add your own personal description. Whatever the case, we must **Stop** in order to gain clarity.

Both Donna and Michael weren't moving and, therefore, felt like they had "stopped" enough already. I want to be clear; like a vehicle, stopping is not the same thing as being stuck. I would like to define exactly what I mean by **Stop** so that there is no confusion.

What we are *not* talking about is:

- Stopping your life
- Quitting your job (at least not yet!)
- Abandoning your obligations

What we are talking about here is about *coasting* for the time being – by coasting, I mean that you must look at your job and the obligations of your life as a punch clock. Start your day by punching in and finish it by punching out. The best illustration I have for this is an attendee, named NK, at one of my live speaking events.

NK couldn't get the results or have the influence he wanted with a Top 50 company. He decided to leave senior management to work in a front-line, customer service job. He knew that he could do more but was unable to attain it in his current department. So, he punched in and punched out every day for two years before the right opportunity came along. I asked him, "Aren't you bored or unhappy? Isn't it time to leave? Don't you feel you are smarter than this?" And his response was an outstanding example of coasting. He said, "I am just coasting while I look for the right opportunity. It's not my favourite thing to do, but I know if I let my thoughts go to a negative place about the value of the work and my contribution that I will not be able to sustain it. Right now, I don't have a choice but to sustain what I am doing until something else comes along."

NK realized that in the meantime he had to show up and do the job he was hired to do. He also understood that by putting significant attention and energy on what wasn't working would cause him to lose the clarity he needed to recognize the right opportunity when it came along.

What I am asking you to do is to sustain judgment for a period of time. If you focus on what is not working and how terrible it currently is, then I promise you, you will not get the results you desire from doing the work in this book. So what do you do instead?

- Show up to do the job you were hired to do
- Refrain from making any life changing decisions (at least until you have finished doing the work in this chapter!)
- Know that this is going to get better
- Stick to the facts about your current situation, and be as objective as you can
- View yourself from the third person perspective as if you were a scientist observing the response to an experiment. There is little to no emotion. Simply observation. If it helps, record what you notice without judgment.

Think of it like surfing. Some waves are smooth, some waves are rough, but once you are out in the ocean, there is a silent resignation to the fact that you can't do anything about it until you get back to shore.

Once you have **Stopped** we can proceed with gaining clarity. We will do this by identifying your current circumstance. This is your "as-is" state (versus your "to-be" state, which we will talk about in Chapter 5 when we get **Moving** again).

In order to gain clarity we will take a look at the whole circumstance. The following are a series of questions and assessments to ensure you are clear about the current state of every aspect of your life. For some, when one thing isn't working in our life it can start to affect other aspects of our lives. For others, the rest of your life is working pretty well and only the career needs some work. I want you to get the job aspect working well while also getting the rest of your life working well too. I have seen instances where, when we get the job rolling, it can affect the other aspects of a person's life. I want your life to work as synergistically as possible – all things working in conjunction with each other so even when there are bumps it doesn't throw us out of our flow state. **For the sake of this book, we have defined flow state as the state in your life where you are performing fully immersed, inspired, and energized.** This is when you experience full enjoyment and involvement in the process of living. This is also what we call a Whole-Life Experience (which we will learn more about in Chapter 8 *Be*).

Grab a new journal and call it "My Whole-Life Experience a Work in Progress" or download the companion workbook at www. ChangeMyLifeCoaching.ca/workbook. Flip to the first page and write a dedication to yourself about how you are going to honour doing the work you need to do. Write about the commitment you are making to yourself and be sure to speak to only putting your own purest, truest voice down on paper.

As you go through the activities in this chapter, I strongly encourage you to remove the voices of your past. Sustain judgment based on what you think to be true. Simply observe.

As best as possible, please objectively rate and describe the following areas of your life. What I mean by objective is: Stick to the facts. Calling your boss a complete jerk isn't objective but saying that you currently don't seem to work well together is objective. I am going to take you through a series of ratings and questions to help you start to gain clarity in your current circumstance. By doing this, you will start to see the whole picture. Only with this will we be able to start *Thinking* about it in a way that allows us to get focused. If you decide to skip this step, I promise, you will continue to be unfulfilled in what you are doing for a living and ultimately unfulfilled in your life. We are going to take a deep and holistic look at your *entire* life.

A word of caution, this book is filled with activities. In fact, it is very action-focused. I understand that you may not feel that you have all of the time in the world to complete this work and you might be telling yourself right now that you don't and that "Christopher doesn't get it because he doesn't know my life". If this happens at any time, I want you to stop working immediately, reach out to me. I'll send you my personal story; it's about overcoming adversity at all costs. No, I don't know your story but I do know adversity and pain and suffering, in deep and intimate ways. I also know that the work you are about to embark on is going to change your life and that it *is* possible!

Okay, let's start to **Stop**!

For each area of your life, indicated below, please rate and answer the following questions. Remember to be like a scientist and simply observe without judgment.

Using the scale below for the following questions:
- 1- *Completely unfulfilled at this time*
- 2- *Somewhat unfulfilled at this time*
- 3- *Somewhat fulfilled at this time*
- 4- *Completely fulfilled at this time*

How would you rate the following areas of your life based on the four-point scale?
- 1- Career/Work
- 2- Money
- 3- Relationships
- 4- Environment – This is about the environment in which you live and work
- 5- Fitness/Health
- 6- Spirituality/Trust – Some people do not consider spirituality as part of their life. If I was to break this down to use it universally let's look at spirituality as having faith. Faith is about trusting. So if you are not spiritual please rate

your current circumstance on your trust for coworkers, relationships, humankind, etc.

7- Mental/Emotional

Answer the following questions for each area of your life about the rating you gave:

1. Why did you give that rating?
2. What are the facts in this area of your life?
3. What factors are causing this to be so?
4. What role have you played in creating this area of your life to be what it is today?
5. What is currently out of your control in this area of your life?
6. What is currently in your control in this area of your life? (The answer is rarely "nothing")
7. Now that you see the state of this area how do you feel about it?

~~~Do this now!~~~

Congratulations! You have now completed a holistic analysis on every area of your life. Completing this exercise will certainly have allowed some themes and patterns to emerge. Make some additional observations in your journal while contemplating the questions below.

1. What did you notice specifically?
2. Which areas are not going so well? Why not? Please answer "Why not" both from a place of external and internal factors.
3. Which areas are working best? (The answer cannot be "none of them" because certainly one, even if it is in a bad state, stands out above the others in that it isn't as bad. If you struggle with this, prioritize the areas as worst to best numbered from 1 to 6.)
4. What makes these areas the best?
5. What links can you see? For example, perhaps you know exactly what you want to do for a living but then when you share it with your spouse they don't encourage the idea. Maybe you believe that your situation won't change unless you have more money... so write down "When I get more money, then I will start my dream business or go back to

school". Maybe your mental state makes you eat poor food and, as a result, you have become overweight and don't feel you perform well at work.

6. Which area, if you work on it first, will help the rest fall into place? Tip: This may or may not be the best or worst area you have listed. Do not base it on the ratings you gave but on your sound judgment.
7. What else do you notice or think needs to be commented on?
8. What else is important to you at this time?
9. What is most important to you at this time?

A word of caution!

Discovering your life's purpose is a spiritual experience. I can't tell you what you will end up doing or being after you go through these activities. I can't even tell you that you will make more money or that when you discover your purpose that it will be an easy journey. What I can tell you is that the most satisfied people in the world are those that end up choosing careers and lives being in service to others. They understand that contribution to making others lives more enjoyable and easier is often the most rewarding thing of all. This is not meant to imply that you will be working in the not-for-profit sector or travelling to third world countries to build houses. It does imply, however, that you can be a bus driver and be in complete service of others. You can be a leader who is more concerned about your staff's wellbeing than you are about your next bonus.

Please keep this in mind as you work your way through this book. You will want to ensure you aren't doing the assessments and activities in this book for the sake of just getting them done. Michael, mentioned earlier, was one of these clients. As we have already learned, he was a go-getter. During his coaching he would do the work and proudly bring it to his sessions. In fact, to date, he was one of my hardest working clients in regards to the effort he put in. He wanted the A+ for completion and got it every single time. However, after a few weeks, Michael wasn't seeing results. This is because Michael was focused only on the completion of the steps, not the analysis or internal introspection, which is what is truly required to have a whole-life experience.

When Michael decided he was going to go beyond just doing the work and actually contribute to his own personal introspection, rather than simply committing to the steps, that was when he started to see results. For Michael, it initially caused him a lot of grief. He realized he had been "doing" for so long that he had missed out on the "enjoying" part of his life. You must connect to the work you are doing on this journey. It's not about the steps; it's about making a deep and personal connection.

Remember the vehicle analogy. A road trip is a wonderful thing but, as we have heard so many times before, *it is not about the destination, it's about the journey.* I want you to be able to enjoy the trip. You won't know what you enjoy if you don't pull over to stop and smell the flowers or, in this case, stop and do the work.

So, did you answer the questions, did you make a connection or have a realization from the previous activity?

If not, go back, take your time!

End of Chapter Reflection

You don't know what you don't know, but now that you know what you know...

> ...What has become more painful? Pain can increase motivation. Pain will cause us to take immediate action and keep us away from more pain or experiencing pain again.

> ...What has become blatantly obvious? Obvious things can also lead us to take easy action—action that is within reach if only we had noticed it before.

> ...What is going to become more rewarding when you get to your destination? Rewards can lead us to take imperfect-inspired action—action that may not be well thought out but gets us moving quickly!

CHAPTER 3

THINK ABOUT WHAT
IS IMPORTANT

Having now completely **Stopped** your vehicle and taken stock of your current state, you now have the opportunity to think about it differently. In the last chapter we have determined the facts of your current situation. Without understanding the facts we can't possibly hope to think about it in a correct way. What we don't really understand at this stage is *why* we are in this current state with our jobs, at least not in a detailed and introspective way. In order to answer this, we must ask ourselves what is *important* about the facts?

Remember, the vehicle still isn't moving at this point, but we are getting close to putting that key back in the ignition. This time, we are going to look at the entire inside and outside of the vehicle to ensure we understand how to operate it correctly in the way that serves our best interests.

As this relates to your career and ultimately your life, we must start to determine your ideal job fit. We have to look beyond passion because passion, while so very important, is fleeting. I am certain you have met people who are exceedingly passionate about many things that should never be a part of their day job. Look at the passion around politics and religion. Those that are exceedingly passionate and outspoken are often the worst people to take on these positions. Passion can be re-introduced when we have a better understanding of the tasks we do from one day to the next. I am not asking you to eliminate passion but rather to put it in the proper perspective that passion can not be everything but one of many factors that should be considered.

At one of my live events, one attendee, Sarah, was stuck on this concept of passion. She was certain that if she didn't start by focusing on passion that she would miss out on her life. The challenge was that she had so much passion in so many areas of her life that she just couldn't quite narrow it all down. At the same event, we had James who could not determine his passions at all and felt that because of this he would never find meaning in his life. He said, "I don't get passionate about anything."

I am reminded of something Marcus Buckingham once said: "Passion isn't something that lives way up in the sky, in abstract dreams and hopes. It lives at ground level, in the <u>specific details of what you're actually doing every day</u>."[7]

> *"Passion isn't something that lives way up in the sky, in abstract dreams and hopes. It lives at ground level, in the specific details of what you're actually doing every day."*
> - Marcus Buckingham

I had Sarah, James, and the rest of the audience take a few moments to write out a shortened version of their own eulogy. A eulogy is the speech that speaks about someone's life and accomplishments, typically at their funeral. We have all heard the statement, "Nobody says, 'I wish I'd have spent more time at work' while lying on their death bed." If we can look at the *ultimate* end, it will provide perspective about the choices we need to be making now in our lives.

Sarah's eulogy sounded like this:

---

[7] Marcus Buckingham quote. (n.d.). Retrieved November 15, 2015, from http://www.brainyquote.com/quotes/quotes/m/marcusbuck526901.html

> *Sarah was a passionate outgoing individual who made a difference in the lives of hundreds of kids. She guided them to look at the world anew, from a place of earthly respect and care. She knew that children truly are our future and if we are going to see a difference in this world that we must start with our children. She would sit down in nature, with children, teaching them the different flowers that were edible and which trees were the best for which kinds of bugs and birds. She showed them that when they were in their darkest, saddest places, they could find grounding in nature and that their confidence and control could come from things like picking up three pieces of garbage whenever they were outside. She made a real difference in the world.*

At this time in her life, Sarah had never worked outside or with children. Do you see that while she mentioned passion in her eulogy, the real meaning came from the day-to-day tasks—the actual things she did to make a difference? She had work that she felt was meaningful; the tasks themselves are what filled her up. Passion fueled this, but she didn't start with passion.

James's eulogy was quite a bit different:

> *James was a family man. He was the first dad in our community who turned off his cell phone every night before he walked in the door, so that his kids could have the first hour of his time. There were days when he was so busy and stressed or sick, but his kids got the very best part of him. One time, when he was working on a big project he noticed how tired he was feeling at the end of every day and he started to shorten the quality time he had reserved for his kids. He found himself saying "I'm too tired" to them when they wanted to play catch outside or a round of MarioKart on the Nintendo. It only took him about a week before he walked into the boss's office, had a very difficult conversation, which lead to a screaming match and a new job within three months to make the adjustments. He was too humble to admit it, but he was the kind of father and man the rest of the community modeled themselves after.*

Again, you can see it was in the small tasks that made the difference. It was the day-to-day activities that filled them up. You can also see an element of their beliefs and values coming out in the eulogy. Beliefs and values hold more credence than passion when it comes to discovering our dream jobs.

I encouraged Sarah and James to continue to write their full eulogy in the following weeks so that they could have a full picture. I also encouraged them to give their eulogy to a couple of friends and mentors with instructions to check up with them every three to six months in order to ensure they were making choices that would align to their eulogy. **The head-fake about writing your eulogy before you die is that it has nothing to do with how you want to die but rather how you want to live**.[8] You can see, in a few short minutes, what was important to both Sarah and James. This, in turn, can dictate how they spend their lives and make choices that are in line with what they ultimately value.

By having a eulogy in place, you only have to make correct choices to get the results you describe. Passion is a part of what both Sarah and James experienced but the subject wasn't about passion itself, instead it was grounded in the specific details of their day-to-day lives.

There are three activities in this chapter that will help us *Think* in an effective way to provide the desired results you are looking for. Thinking is about turning over every stone, exploring your thoughts. Thinking does not imply that action is required at this time. It will also answer the question what is important, provide focus, and ultimately provide you with a filter to make decisions that you can use for the rest of your life for any job or task you are presented with.

The first activity is to write your own personal eulogy and give it to a friend; the second is to identify your values and beliefs and analyze which are working for you and which are not; and the third will be an

---

[8] Head-fake: occurs when someone is taught a deeper lesson under the pretense of learning something simple. For example, while learning to make your bed as a child you are also being taught discipline, organization, and responsibility.

extensive look at your day-to-day activities at a detailed level using a five-step process I call "Going Beyond Your Passion: Discovering Your Job Fit". I promise, by the time you are done this work, you will know exactly why you have been floundering with your career choices and you will know exactly what is painful. You will also know exactly the pieces you need to focus on because they put you in your very best state of mind!

You might be saying by now that, "Wait, there is more work?". Yes, because it is a journey. This is what happens as you begin to peel back the layers. The answers don't come overnight. You may be in a position where you have spent so much time looking for the answers, that perhaps you have tried a number of quick fix, Band-Aid solutions, which ultimately left you just as confused and in the same position. This book should be kept with you for your entire life. You should reference it when things get dark or change for you in your life. Initially you may do all of the activities, which I strongly encourage you to do if you'd like to finally get this resolved. In time, you will revisit some of this work as things change for you in your life. Consider this the map for your vehicle. Sometimes roads change, sometimes they are blocked temporarily for construction, and sometimes they are changed forever. These activities are intended to give you the flexibility you need to be successful no matter where you are in your life. They provide you with the fluidity in those moments where the road ahead seems blocked without a clear and present detour.

Write Your Eulogy

A good eulogy talks about both the big things and the little things that mattered to the person. It speaks to the unique things that make this person who they were. They are positive and confident. They stay away from the dark side of a person and focus on what made them great. They provide inspiration in things that rekindle old memories, stories, or feelings towards the person to whom they are written about. The tone can be warm, sad, insightful and thoughtful, or my personal favourite, humorous. Ultimately, they show a reflection of who this person truly was and how they spent their life.

Take a few moments now and write your eulogy. Don't worry about being brief. Focus on what you know for certain you would like said about you at your funeral. This means that you will be future thinking about the life you want to live as well as referencing the life you have already lived so far. You might contemplate some of the below questions:

1. What was neat, fun and quirky about you?
2. How did you change the lives of the people around you?
3. What did you make people feel and how did you make people feel that way?
4. What was your contribution to the world?
5. What are some of the unique stories about you that really speak to the kind of character and person you were? Think about what has already happened and especially think about the future stories you'd like to create that haven't happened yet.
6. What was the one thing in your life you absolutely had to do before you died?
7. What was the thing you struggled with forever but were eventually able to look at in a humorous way?
8. What are the anecdotal things, the things everybody knew to be fundamentally true about you?
9. What would your best friend say about you?
10. What experiential learning did you have? What learning did you have that simply came from living life. This is learning that you have from your own stories and hearing other people's stories. This is learning that comes from not allowing your experiences to stay in silos but rather combining lessons and learning you have had to find new ways of thinking about achieving your goals and overcoming obstacles.

Regarding question eight, there is an example that comes to mind from my grandma's funeral:

"When Lynn had her nose in a book you couldn't interrupt her. It wasn't that you couldn't try but simply that when she was reading she was so absorbed in her book that she wouldn't even notice you. Smoke alarms could be

going off in the house and she would still be reading her
book with a half-smile on her face."

You see how much you can learn about how Lynn wanted to spend
her time. You can see, from this one example, what she valued in
her life.

By doing this activity you will start to understand what you are truly
passionate about but more importantly you will understand the
activities you must do in order to truly live your passion.

Once you have this into a state that is "good enough" you must pass
it to two friends and two mentors who are going to check in with you
every six months to see if you are on track. This doesn't mean that
things can't change but you now have built in accountability.

Determine Your Values & Beliefs Surrounding Work & Life

Now that you have a eulogy you are getting a good idea about what
is truly important to you. Now you must outline your values and
beliefs about work and life. Be sure to use your workbook or journal.

Values are the things that you determine to be useful or important.
These are the things you consider to be worthwhile. Ultimately it is
how you operate, your principles.

Beliefs are essentially a big piece of your blueprint. This is what you
learned growing up and how you grew up. This is what you believe
to be true as a result of your history and significant experiences in
your life.

These things together could be referred to as your M.O. or modus
operandi.[9] Essentially this is the way you do something, your
characteristic methods.

---

[9] Modus operandi: a particular way or method of doing something, especially one
that is characteristic or well established.

This is important because we sometimes end up with conflicting values and beliefs. Some examples of conflicts could be:

- Stealing bread for your starving family
- Loving your boss but seeing him do something unethical
- Earning a living with a steady job versus taking a risk to do something you absolutely love
- Needing to have a new job with a pay cheque before you quit the one you currently have

Now, take stock of your values for work and life. To do this you might answer the questions: What do you *value* at work based on what you have seen about you from your past? And, What do you *value* in your personal life based on what you have seen about you from your past? Then replace the word "value" with the phrase "believe to be ultimately true" in the two questions above.

Once you have done this look at your values and see which ones might have conflicts. Be honest, not all of the values you grew up with are serving who you are today.

Finally, what values and beliefs would you like to change by replacing them with something more useful? What will you replace them with? We have to replace them because trying to just get rid of them usually doesn't work. For example, maybe you have a belief that you will always struggle with money. It is difficult to simply remove this belief from your brain, it's much easier to correct it with something similar but truer. It could look like this:

> Original belief: "I will always struggle with money."

> Revised belief: "I have struggled with money up to this point; however, I can't predict the future and will make much better decisions moving forward."

Once you have done this activity you will be able to see if this is where the current problem is in your life. You should be able to determine if it is actually the company that is the problem, the people you work with, or your own perception and approach to your work.

You may wish to make some additional notes in your journal or workbook about what themes have come up for you. What have you observed?

There is one piece missing though, isn't there? What about the actual job itself? In the next chapter you are going to discover your job fit. This is a deep-dive, five-step activity that promises to dissect every part of how you operate in order to become clear on what kinds of jobs you will want to begin exploring.

End of Chapter Reflection

You don't know what you don't know, but now that you know what you know:

...What has now become more painful?
...Therefore, what is an action you have been avoiding that you now need to take?

...What has now become blatantly obvious?
...Therefore, what is an easy action that is right in front of you that you can take right now?

...What is going to become more rewarding now?
...Therefore, what is an action that you have always wanted to take that you just haven't gotten around to?

CHAPTER 4

GOING BEYOND YOUR PASSION: DISCOVERING YOUR JOB FIT

In this chapter we are going to literally break down the activities you have done up to this point in your life. I strongly encourage you to take your time with this portion of the book. By the end of this activity you will end up with three to five Job Fit Filters each for things that put you in your peak state and weak state. You will be able to use these to run through any job or task to ensure you stay fulfilled in all of your careers, no matter what changes around you.

One of my one-on-one coaching clients, Sam, said, "Where was this when I was in high school? I have spent so much of my life doing things that put me in my weak state. Now I know exactly what I need to focus on!" He was so validated that tears of joy were streaming down his face.

If you require an example about how to approach this next section, I encourage you to go to www.ChangeMyLifeCoaching.ca/workbook where we provide you a sample of each of these five steps.

Step 1: Dissecting the Parts

Grab your résumé, the most recent one you have will do. It does not need to be up-to-date. If you don't have a résumé, don't worry about making one at this time. You can simply start with what you remember or know. The résumé is simply meant to trigger your memory about the tasks you have done. Please read all of the instructions for Step 1 prior to starting this activity.

What you are going to do is separate the tasks you have done into three separate columns or three separate pages: 1) Peak State Tasks, 2) Neutral State Tasks, and 3) Weak State Tasks. You can use the workbook on our website or you can use word processing software.

In Column 1: Write down your "Peak State Tasks"

These are activities and tasks that put you in your peak state, meaning that when you do them, you feel strong and full of energy. They fill you up and you want more of these things in your day. These should be things from work, hobbies, etc.

Do not worry if you are not good at these things yet. We only care if they fill you up at this time. For example, if every time you speak in public you feel wonderful or empowered, it belongs in this column even if you are not very good at it yet.

To determine if something should go in this section you might ask yourself, "Is this something I love doing or hate doing?" Then, "Do I love or hate that whole task or just part of it? Which parts?" Put the parts you love in this column and the parts you don't in one of the other columns. For example, you might love plumbing when it's a new home construction but you might hate it when it is fixing existing plumbing that was built years ago. These are important distinctions.

Focus on how you feel, do not think about what it will take to get there if you aren't good at it and do not focus on job titles. Simply focus on the most important tasks you have done to this point in your life. Be specific and break it down.

For example, you might say, "organization" – what does this mean? Organizing what puts you in your Peak State? Is it organizing files, basements, or events that puts you in your peak state? Stick to the stuff you have done. Don't future think about what you *might* like.

In Column 2: Write down your "Neutral State Tasks"

In this column, write down activities and tasks that you feel neutral about. These tasks neither put you in your Peak State nor your Weak State. If you had more or less of these tasks it would be inconsequential to you. Be careful, this column should be used sparingly. You should have fewer items in this column than in any of the other columns.

In Column 3: Write down your "Weak State Tasks"

In this column, write down activities and tasks that put you in a weak state. This means that when you do them you feel weak or drained. They do not fill you up and you want less of these things in your day.

Do not worry if you are good at these things. We only care if they drain you up at this time.

For example, if every time you do data entry, you feel drained or bored then it belongs in this column, even if you are incredible at it! There are a lot of things we are good at that shouldn't be part of our day-to-day work.

To determine if something should go in this section you might ask yourself is this something I love doing or hate doing? Then, do I love or hate that whole task or just part of it? Which parts? Put the parts you hate in this column and the parts you don't hate in one of the other columns.

Remember our plumbing example? Here you would put "Fix existing plumbing that is plugged or broken", while you still have "Fitting new homes with brand new plumbing" in your Peak State column.

Focus on how you feel, do not think about what it will take to get rid of these tasks and do not focus on job titles. Simply focus on the most important tasks you have done to this point in your life.

In order to effectively complete this activity you will want to consider:

- Your current or most recent job
- Any previous jobs you have held
- Your hobbies and interests
- Your previous schooling and education (There are little nuggets everywhere you look. In one example, my client didn't bother to look at her high school education because it had been twenty years since she had been to school so it didn't seem relevant. When we finally looked back we realized that she loved her biology homework the most and it was the homework she always did first. Is it any surprise that she is now happily employed as a physio-therapist?)

The idea behind this activity is not to discover a job title or what you are good at, but rather to determine what puts you in your Peak State versus what puts you in your Weak State.

A Few Tips

Remember, if you are using your résumé, you may have put three or four bullet points about what you did for each job, however, we know we do more than three or four things in those jobs. For example, you might have said that you completed "Closing Duties" in a retail store. We know that closing duties might include completing inventory, doing a cash-out, merchandizing and organizing the store for the next day. Each of these tasks may have put you in a peak, neutral, or weak state. In this case, you will need to dig deeper than what is on your résumé.

Do NOT use this section to talk about the types of people that put you in a peak or weak state or the company's fit with your own values. Those are things that can be identified with your values and beliefs in the previous chapter. This section is specifically for the tasks that you do from one day to the next.

This activity can take some time so be sure to take your time with it. If you are having a hard time looking into your past to determine what puts you in your Peak, Neutral, and Weak states then consider keeping a journal or a notebook at work. You can use this to track each task throughout your day that puts you in your peak, neutral, or weak state. Don't simply stop at your current job though. You have a whole history of tasks that you will want to take a look at. When you are finished this step you could have a number of pages. You will want to be detailed and robust in your thinking.

Example of Step 1

Peak State Tasks	Neutral State Tasks	Weak State Tasks
I want more of these tasks. They make me feel strong and put me in my peak state.	*Having more or less of these tasks doesn't really affect me at this time in my life.*	*I want less of these tasks. They drain me and put me in my weak state.*
Planning and organizing schedules	Writing emails	Data entry
Developing agendas for meetings and events	Writing corporate communications	Correcting others' mistakes
Brainstorming ideas for company events	Doing math homework	Editing my boss's reports
Acting in plays	*Etc.*	Public speaking without a plan when improvisation is required
Public speaking where I have time to rehearse		Building stage sets
Reading books on subjects I'm interested in		*Etc.*
Etc.		
These three lists will be quite long depending on your previous experience.		

Step 2: Peak State versus Pastimes

Please read all of the instructions for Step 2 prior to starting this activity. Now go through all of the Peak State tasks you listed and for each item you have listed and ask yourself the following:

Can I see myself doing what it takes to get better at this task to make a living, even if it is on a part-time basis?

If the answer is "no" then write it on a separate page that you have labeled as "Pastimes". Think of these things as hobbies. For example, maybe you love to cook. When you cook, it fills you up and maybe you'd even like more of it in your day. This means it would have been placed on your "Peak State" column. However, perhaps you love experimenting with making new meals but you aren't interested in really doing what it takes to get to the next professional level in order to make a living at it. In this case, cooking would be a pastime. Cross it off your "Peak State" column and write it down on your "Pastimes" page.

> *"It may be important to explore your pastimes with a Career Coach. Some of them might end up being your dream job."*
> - Christopher Lawrence

It may be important to explore "Pastimes" with a Career Coach because there are exceptions to these criteria. For example, one woman had "knitting" and "yarn" as a pastime but then realized that when she focused on it solely, blogged about it, absorbed it, ate, breathed, and dreamt about knitting and yarn she was able to successfully turn it into her full-time job.[10]

---

[10] Vaynerchuk, Gary. *Crush It!*. [New York]: HarperStudio, 2009. Print.

Example of Step 2

Peak State Tasks	Neutral State Tasks	Weak State Tasks
I want more of these tasks. They make me feel strong and put me in my peak state	*Having more or less of these tasks doesn't really affect me at this time in my life.*	*I want less of these tasks. They drain me and put me in my weak state.*
Planning and organizing schedules	Writing emails	Data entry
Developing agendas for meetings and events	Writing corporate communications	Correcting other's mistakes
Brainstorming ideas for company events	Doing math homework	Editing my boss's reports
~~Acting in plays~~	*Etc.*	Public speaking without a plan when improvisation is required
Public speaking where I have time to rehearse		*Etc.*
~~Reading books on subjects I'm interested in~~		
Etc.		
The crossed out items have been moved into the Pastimes section below.	*Do not use the shaded areas for this step*	

Pastimes
These are tasks that put me in a peak state but ones that I am not really willing to spend a lot of time, money, or effort to become a professional, nor am I willing to spend a lot of time, money, or effort to get good enough to make a living doing these things.
Acting in Plays   Reading books on subjects I'm interested in   *Etc.*

Step 3: Categorize Your Peak & Weak State Tasks

You are now going to go back to your Peak and Weak State Tasks (with your pastimes removed) and put them into categories. You can set the Pastimes and Neutral State tasks aside now. You will not require them moving forward now that they have been filtered out but be sure to refer back to them when you find yourself craving more fulfillment or work/life balance. Pastimes are still activities that can fill you up, it's just that they aren't activities and tasks you intend to earn a living with. Please read all of the instructions for Step 3 prior to starting this activity.

To put your Peak State Tasks into categories you might see that you have:

- Planning schedules
- Developing agendas
- Brainstorming ideas for company events

All of these could be placed under a category called "Event Planning". You will still want to list the three bullets under the heading to keep the information organized.

You may also see you have some items that fall in two categories. For example, you might end up with a category called "Administrative" and one called "Accounting". Underneath both of these you could have a bullet point called "data-entry". It is okay to have one bullet fall under many categories. In fact it's important in discovering your Job Fit, so where it makes sense list a bullet point multiple times! Remember, do not include your pastimes within these categories.

Example of Step 3

Remember this? It is the information that remains after Step 1 and 2. Obviously yours will be a significantly longer list but for demonstration purposes the below will do.

Peak State Tasks *I want more of these tasks. They make me feel strong and put me in my peak state.*	**Weak State Tasks** *I want less of these tasks. They drain me and put me in my weak state.*
Planning and organizing schedules	Data entry
Developing agendas for meetings and events	Correcting other's mistakes
Brainstorming ideas for company events	Editing my boss's reports
~~Acting in plays~~	Public speaking without a plan when improvisation is required
Public speaking where I have time to rehearse	*Etc.*
~~Reading books on subjects I'm interested in~~	
Etc.	

You will create a new table to put this into categories. Categories are bolded and the tasks are listed underneath.

Peak State Categories	Weak State Categories
These are the categories for tasks that put me in a peak state, which I will use to create my job fit filters.	*These are the categories for tasks that put me in a weak state, which I will use to create my job fit filters.*
Event Planning	**Event Planning**
Planning and organizing schedules	Public speaking without a plan when improvisation is required
Developing agendas for meetings and events	**Detailed Work**
Brainstorming ideas for company events	Data entry
	Correcting other's mistakes
Public speaking where I have time to rehearse	Editing my boss's reports
	Etc.
Administrative	
Planning and organizing schedules	
Developing agendas for meetings and events	
Etc.	
You can see that we have some tasks listed twice under different categories.	*You can see that Event Planning has some tasks that put this person in a Peak State and a Weak State depending on how they are required to execute the task.*

I have deliberately not provided categories for you. This is because it is all based on your unique perception. You may have tasks that you would put under "Project Management" or "Blue Collar" while someone else might put those under headings like "Event Planning" or "Home Projects" respectively. Additionally, you could have as little as three or as many as fifteen categories depending on your previous experience and how detailed you were in Step 1 of this chapter. If I provide you with categories then I am limiting the areas that you may think about on your own or I could completely change the way you think about the work you have previously done. This may inhibit your personal growth and satisfaction. If you think a category belongs, then it needs to be there!

Please ensure you don't leave out any of the tasks you listed from Step 1. Everything you have listed should belong to at least one category. You may have a couple of tasks that are stand-alone items which end up being their own category. This is perfectly fine as long as nothing is left behind from Step 1.

Step 4: Making Observations

Now that you have categorized your Peak and Weak State Tasks you are probably noticing some themes emerging based on your observations. Capture these themes on a separate page called "Observations For Tasks I Have Completed". For example, you might see that for certain categories you love repetitive daily tasks because it allows you to compete with yourself or gives you the ability to not take work home at the end of the day. You might make an observation about this by saying "I notice that I love repetitive tasks where I get to compete with myself". This step requires a little bit of intuition. Please read all of the instructions for Step 4 prior to starting this activity.

Continuing our Example for Step 4 based on what we did in Steps 1, 2 and 3.

Observations for Tasks I Have Completed	
Peak State Observations *In the last three steps, I have noticed these themes about things I like doing*	**Weak State Observations** *In the last three steps, I have noticed these themes about things I DO NOT like doing*
I realized while doing Step 3 that I really enjoy working with a small group of people to brainstorm company events and execute them. I realized that I completely love serving my boss's needs when she has requests of me, particularly having control of her schedule. *Etc.*	I noticed that I don't like taking the lead on planning the events. I work best when someone gives me direction. Based on what I saw in Steps 1 and 3, I realized that I HATE doing detailed work where I am forced to be meticulous. *Etc.*
This step will really help you put together your Job Fit filters in Step 5.	

Other examples of this could include:

- "I realize now that most of my job has to do with reaching out to clients to make cold calls. I love selling but I hate making the cold calls."
- "It is obvious to me now that most of what fills me up really involves the arts and not much of my job gives me this kind of creativity."
- "OMG! It's obvious to me that I COMPLETELY HATE fixing other peoples mistakes! I want to be the creator of things… not the fixer!"

Step 5: Creating Your Uniquely Customized Job Fit Filters

By this point you have:

1. Identified what you currently know puts you in your Peak and Weak States
2. Extracted your Pastimes
3. Categorized all of your tasks into themes
4. Made important observations

This information alone is invaluable!

Now you are ready to create your Job Fit Filters. What you will do is create three to five statements each for your Peak and Weak State information. In order to do this, you are going to refine all of your previous work into a digestible filter that you can use every single day when you are asked to complete a new task or are considering a new job. I encourage you to read all of Step 5 before proceeding with creating your filters.

To do this activity, you will need to brainstorm and use creativity. Do not expect perfection the first time (or ever). You will need to allow your filters to evolve not only through this process but also through your life. This is because you will have new experiences as your life continues. New experiences can make you want to tweak your filters. This is important. Allow it to happen!

To start, look at the categories you created and observations you have made. For example, you might see that you have "Project Management" as a category and you have another category called "Planning". You also notice that you have made an observation that you like "to start new things". For illustration purposes let's look at it like a math equation:

Category: Project Management
+
Category: Planning
+
Observation: I like to start new things

You can now start to tie these things together into a filter, which could be worded as such:

= *"Kicking off and planning new projects in areas that I love"*

You can see in this filter we have covered our bases with the information we were provided above. What about that very vague part "...in areas that I love"? Because you have done all of the detailed work previously on what puts you in your peak, neutral, and weak states you now know the areas that you love and hate intimately. If you ever forget, you can go back and look at them. To an outsider, this statement might be very vague, but you will know exactly what specific tasks could fall into that part of the statement.

Another example:

You might have categories that say "accounts payable" and "sending invoices" and you might have a theme that speaks to your "distaste for repetitive tasks".

Category: Accounts Payable
+
Category: Sending Invoices
+
Observation: Distaste for repetitive tasks
=
Job Fit Filter: *"Doing daily repetitive tasks that involve numbers and have no personal meaning for me"*

This could also be stated as:

"Doing too many tasks that involve data entry where I see no personal connection"

Or

"Doing too many detailed tasks that require extreme accuracy where it does not feel like my contribution matters."

Whatever filters you come up with, you will want to give yourself a few days to ensure the statements are appropriately truthful, vulnerable, and robust. Make sure that your Job Fit Filters have captured ALL of your bullet points, categories, and observations. If we leave something out, then you stand the risk of continuing to be dissatisfied.

Once you have created these you will want to ensure you allow them to evolve. What I mean by this is that you will continue to have experiences in your life and try new tasks. When this happens, it could adjust your filters over time. You will want to revisit this work occasionally if you are feeling unfulfilled in your job.

For example, I used to have a filter that said "Making a plan to overcome obstacles in areas I'm comfortable with" and it was perfectly accurate when I first wrote it, but as I had more experiences (experiential learning), I was able to refine it to say "Brainstorming ideas in areas I'm passionate about in order to bust obstacles that get in the way of people and businesses achieving their dreams". You can see the core of my filter is the same (it's about overcoming obstacles) but the second one is more specific and truer for me at this time in my life.

By the way, when I read that statement I am filled with joy. It excites me! Any job I do, any task I am asked to take on – if it meets this filter then I know it's going to be a good fit and very likely on the path to maintaining my dream job. If you feel this, then you know you are hitting the mark with your Job Fit Filters.

> *"Allow your Job Fit Filters to evolve as you evolve.*
> *This will ensure you continue to have a Whole-Life Experience!"*
> - Christopher Lawrence

Continuing with our example from Steps 1, 2, 3, and 4

This is the information from Step 3

Peak State Categories *These are the categories for tasks that put me in a Peak State, which I will use to create my Job Fit Filters.*	Weak State Categories *These are the categories for tasks that put me in a Weak State, which I will use to create my Job Fit Filters.*
Event Planning Planning and organizing schedules Developing agendas for meetings and events Brainstorming ideas for company events Public speaking where I have time to rehearse **Administrative** Planning and organizing schedules Developing agendas for meetings and events *Etc.*	**Detailed Work** Data entry Correcting others' mistakes Editing my boss' reports **Event Planning** Public speaking without a plan when improvisation is required *Etc.*

This is the information from Step 4

Observations for Tasks I Have Completed	
Peak State Observations *In the last three steps, I have noticed these themes about things I like doing*	**Weak State Observations** *In the last three steps, I have noticed these themes about things I DO NOT like doing*
I realized while doing Step 3 that I really enjoy working with a small group of people to brainstorm company events and execute them. I realized that I completely love serving my boss's needs when she has requests of me, particularly having control of her schedule. *Etc.*	I noticed that I don't like taking the lead on planning the events. I work best when someone gives me direction. Based on what I saw in Steps 1 and 3, I realized that I HATE doing detailed work where I am forced to be meticulous. *Etc.*

We will now use the information from Step 3 and Step 4 to create job fit filters

Peak State Filters *I will ensure any new tasks or jobs I decide to try will meet these filters at least 80% of the time.*	**Weak State Filters** *I will ensure any new tasks or jobs I decide to try will meet these filters NO MORE THAN 20% of the time.*
Category: Event Planning + Category: Administrative + Observation: I realized while doing Step 3 that I really enjoy working with a small group of people to brainstorm company events and execute them.	Category: Detailed Work + Theme: Based on what I saw in Steps 1 and 3 I realized that I HATE doing detailed work where I am forced to be meticulous. = **Weak State Job Fit Filter 1: Doing detailed work where meticulous accuracy is required.**

= **Peak State Job Fit Filter 1: Working with a small team of people to plan, organize, and execute company events especially where I get to be a presenter or facilitator.** Category: Administrative **+** Observation: I realized that I completely love serving my boss's needs when she has requests of me, particularly having control of her schedule. **=** **Peak State Job Fit Filter 2: Acting as a gatekeeper for my leader's time and space.** *Etc.*	Category: Event Planning **+** Theme: I noticed that I don't like taking the lead on planning the events. I work best when someone gives me direction. **=** **Weak State Job Fit Filter 2: Being a manager or leader of things, especially when there is no structured plan in place.** *Etc.*

You will want 3 to 5 filters for both Peak and Weak states each. If there are less than 3 each, then you may have combined too many categories and themes. If there are more than 5 each it may mean there is overlap or it is too complex. When you are done you should have 6 to 10 filters total.

In our examples we have created four statements or Job Fit Filters total. Let's run a couple of scenarios so that you can see how to use the filters.

Scenario 1

Let's assume the person with the filter above wanted a complete career change and wanted to be an electrician. We don't quite have enough information to judge this accurately but based on the information we do have, we can make an educated guess.

To be an electrician you must understand diagrams and details. In some cases you will need to troubleshoot problems that exist. Based on the limited information we have about this person and using their filters, I would suggest they would not be a good fit for this position for a few reasons.

While the day-to-day tasks of an Electrician require a lot of structure (which we know this person wants), they do not prefer detailed, meticulous work. As an electrician putting the wrong wire in the wrong place could be detrimental – in other words, detailed work is required. Additionally, even if this person had a filter that spoke to liking many aspects of the work of an electrician, they still wouldn't have the opportunity to manage schedules and plan events. This means that they wouldn't be operating within at least two of their Peak State Job Fit Filters. That's a huge miss! You want your day-to-day activities to meet as many of your filters as possible.

Scenario 2

Let's continue to assume this person wanted a complete career change but this time they wanted to be an Assistant Daycare Employee. At this time, we don't know how they feel about children. This may or may not be captured in one of their other filters, however, we could assume that Daycare employees aren't required to do a lot of meticulous, detailed tasks. Also, this position is an Assistant Daycare Employee, which means they are not in charge of the operation but rather following the lead of someone else. Those two things seem to avoid the Weak State Job Fit Filters.

Looking at the Peak State Job Fit Filters, this person would likely get to work with all of the other employees to plan events for the children and probably even get the chance to present or facilitate to the children through story-telling or activities. They would not have the opportunity to be a gatekeeper of their manager's schedule though. This could be addressed in other ways like being the gatekeeper for the children's schedule (i.e. nap time, snack time, play time, etc.). Those things may or may not meet this persons needs because it would look quite different than what they are doing now.

Based on this information we might suggest that it isn't a terrible fit, it might even be a good fit for this person and it's certainly worth exploring. To explore it they might do some volunteer work with children to see if this fills them up.

Additional Instructions for Step 5

A word of caution! Sometimes we get stuck in the wording of creating a "perfect" statement. DO NOT DO THIS! Simply allow this to flow and go with "it's good enough for now". You can come back later and tweak your statements. The concern is if you spend too much time wording it, your focus becomes more about creating the statement than trying it out and living it!

When you are done this activity, you will have created at least three Job Fit Filters and you might have as many as five for each of your Peak State and Weak State. If you have less than three filters, then I am concerned that you have not captured all of your bullet points, categories, and themes from your previous work. If you have more than five filters on each side, then I am concerned that your filters will become cumbersome when you are trying to use them. There are likely two statements that you can combine into one if that is the case.

Another word of caution! Do not force yourself to have five statements if three or four will do the same job. If you are like me then you will see "five" and force yourself to fill them in because you want an A+ for doing the work (remember Michael from the previous chapter?). It is more important for you to focus on making a connection to the work rather than filling in all of the blanks!

Be patient with yourself. These may not (and likely won't) come out perfect the first time. Adopt the mantra "good enough for now", test them on a few tasks or job descriptions to see how they work and then come back and evolve them as needed.

Once you have done this, you will want to keep your job fit filters close by until you know them off by heart (not from memory, but from personal clarity in that you know them well enough that it is clear to you when a new task or job offer comes up that you know very quickly which questions to ask to determine if it fits within your job fit filters). If you are a job seeker, then you need to have these committed to your soul so that when you are interviewing your new potential employer, you can ask meaningful questions that will provide you with the clearest possible picture about what you will actually do in that role from one day to the next.

Once you have these filters you will want to start to make adjustments to your day where you are operating at least 80% of your time on the Peak State Tasks. In order to do this, you will need to learn to influence and negotiate with your boss and those around you. Many people believe that they have no ability to do this. If this is the case, you must remember that this is a fundamental skill that you are doing all of the time, whether you realize it or not. Some simply do it consciously and competently. For others it's unconscious and incompetent. If this is something you struggle with, you may wish to explore our online training programs or a combination of online, phone, or in-person coaching programs where we teach people this skill.

End of Chapter Reflection

You don't know what you don't know, but now that you know what you know:

...What has now become more painful?
...Therefore, what is an action you have been avoiding that you now need to take?

...What has now become blatantly obvious?
...Therefore, what is an easy action that is right in front of you that you can take right now?

...What is going to become more rewarding now?
...Therefore, what is an action that you have always wanted to take that you just haven't gotten around to?

CHAPTER 5

MOVE ONLY AFTER SETTING YOUR DIRECTION

Do you feel ready to start driving your vehicle again? At this point we have come to a full *Stop* to take stock and identify the facts about our current situation. We already answered where we were on our own personal highway. We gained clarity. This allowed us to *Think* so that we could discover our current state. This ultimately allowed us to focus on what is really important and possible. Now, we are finally at a place where we can *Move*. In other words we can now set a direction. We will start by locking in a destination into our GPS and start driving again. Maybe very slowly at first if you are more pragmatic about it. Although, you might come shooting out of the gate because now you feel ready!

I strongly recommend that you read Chapter 5 and 6 one after the other before doing any of the activities outlined in each chapter.

When I work with my clients one-on-one, in groups, and at my live speaking events, I usually see a lot of "engine revving" by this point. People have finally discovered what it is that is painful to them and it is becoming much clearer that they want to get out of that place. They are ready to get going!

In order to get going we don't want to just start speeding down the freeway of life without at least having some impression of a direction that we should start moving. This chapter is all about setting a direction and aligning you to get to that destination in the most direct route possible. Without this direction, we can end up with a few false starts. Using the information from the last two chapters, it will become apparent to you where you need to start and it might not be where you thought you would start. We are going to answer the question "What are the steps?".

Holland was one of the clients that worked with me in one of our smaller groups for a couple of years. She, like the others, came to the group looking to discover her dream job. The group went through a process similar to the one you are going through in this book. When it came time to pick her destination she was raring to go. She made several outstanding steps on her journey but ended up landing a job that wasn't quite where she wanted to be. This can happen to anyone. What was unique about Holland, though, was that she was sort of jumping all over the place. We had to get her to **Stop** and **Think** again. Not to the detail we have already experienced, but simply tweaking the work that was already there. This allowed her to gain some additional clarity.

Eventually, what Holland discovered was that she was trying to find a deeper connection to people and she wasn't finding it no matter where she went to work. I asked her what that *connection* might look, feel or sound like and she described having friends over for dinner and games or to watch a movie. This clearly had almost nothing to do with her working environment but it certainly affected her perception of her working environment. I probed further and it came out that she wasn't proud of the place she lived in and she also wasn't happy with her personal appearance. For Holland, this is when she finally got on the right road. She was able to work on her fitness and began getting her house organized and presentable for guests. It was a long journey for her but one that was rich with rewards and absolutely necessary for her to experience satisfaction in her career.

The point that I am trying to make is that sometimes we will set a direction for our career but then we must align the rest of ourselves to that direction as well. With this, comes challenges and false starts. There is a *knowing* that must come from deciding when we are on the wrong road and therefore must **Stop** and **Think** again, versus *knowing* when we have only hit a few roadblocks but must stay on our current course. The only way to determine this is through trial and error. But by following the activities outlined in this chapter, you will have a much better idea about which direction you choose to **Move** in order to get the best possible results for your career and life.

We are going to start with short-term vision for a few reasons:

- As humans we are best motivated by creating short-term goals with many rewards along the way
- If we start with something easy it will build our confidence. Sometimes we feel we have to overcome our greatest challenge and then we will be able to take on anything. There could be some truth to this; however, to create sustainable, lasting change we are better served by starting with short easy bursts. This allows us to see that we can achieve something. Then we start to feel confident so we can go bigger and bigger!

In time, you will be able to create a long-term vision for your whole life and you will be able to work on two or three visions at the same time that all lead to your ultimate goals. You can do all of that using the steps outlined below. For now, start with one short-haul, easy-to-get-to destination and when you achieve it you will celebrate it to lock in those good feelings. Then choose another to work on. Once you are able to get to a few short-haul destinations you will have a good rhythm and you will be able to take on more. Now let's start moving!

Setting Your Direction: Creating a Vision

What we were looking at in Chapter 2 when we **Stopped** was your current state, also known as your "*as-is*" state. Now, we are going to look at your desired end state, also known as your "*to-be*" state. For one area of your life, you are going to answer the question "What does finished look like?".

To answer this question you will want to pull together and review the following items:

1. In Chapter 2 you identified which area of your life, if you worked on it first, would help the rest fall into place. Perhaps after some contemplation, and the additional work you have done up to this point, you will want to adjust your first priority. Perhaps you will stick with what you have originally written in your journal or workbook. Either way, now is the time to go back and take a look at that work and see what came forward. This is where you will need to start.

2. You will also want to review your eulogy from the Chapter 3 entitled "Think About What's Important". There may be little nuggets in your eulogy, perhaps something small and easy you can start to achieve right now, today! Something that you could choose to start a short-term vision with.

3. Review these pieces and determine what part of your life you'd like to work on. It should be something you can achieve quite quickly. Some examples for your first try might include:

   - Having the conversation with your boss that you have been avoiding
   - Hitting the next sales goal
   - Going out to a networking event that you never would have normally attended previously

   Or, if your first priority isn't work related, like it wasn't for my client Holland, then you might consider starting with something else like:

   - Losing five or ten pounds
   - Taking a flying lesson
   - Getting your driver's license

What don't usually make good short-haul destinations (mainly because they may be too big to achieve right out of the gate) are things like the following:

- Losing 150 pounds
- Getting a degree
- Getting a 30% raise

It's not that these things aren't achievable. In fact, they are quite achievable, but we lose our momentum quickly when the destination seems too far away. So while you might want these things, break them down into smaller bite-sized chunks. This will create good patterns and build your confidence.

4. Create a compelling and inspiring vision. A simple statement that excites you and gives you direction. Remember, don't get stuck on the wording. You can tweak the words as time passes. Instead, focus on the result you are trying to achieve, which is to create momentum.

Good visions are ones that you can remember. When you hear them, they inspire you and hold you to your principles. They have an element of contribution to something outside of who you are as a person. This is because we are rewarded when we contribute to something outside of ourselves and quite often we will do more for others than we will for ourselves. Additionally, visions very clearly and specifically define our desired end state. Some examples of a good vision might be:

"Finally talking to my boss about a personal development plan to move into a leadership position where I will be able to give back to my staff and be fulfilled by the day-to-day tasks that come with that role."

"Losing ten pounds so I can have more energy to play with my kids and to be the example I know my family needs."

> *"Turning off my cell phone before I walk into the house so
> that my spouse gets the first five minutes of my undivided
> attention. This will make my relationship more enjoyable
> for years to come!"*

You can see that these all tie into a bigger vision, a bigger result, but can be very easily attained in the short-term. All of these are specific about what they do. For some, they will be compelling and inspiring. They all have an element of contribution outside of the person who has set them.

Now you might be a bit like Dale. Dale was at one of my speaking events and he came up to me after the event and said, "I've heard this crap about creating a vision a thousand times before and no matter how many times I have set them they haven't stuck". Dale has a very good point! If it were just about setting a vision we would be at our destination already, wouldn't we?

Dale and I spoke for a few minutes and I invited him to come into my office for a strategy session, where we could get into the details surrounding what types of visions he was setting and why they weren't sticking.

When he came to me, we discovered that while Dale's visions were generally good. It was when I asked him about how he executed them that we saw the flaw. He didn't have good practices that supported the vision. Without good practices your vehicle runs out of fuel very quickly. This is why only about 8% of people ever see their New Year's Resolutions come to fruition.[11] We must put in place daily practices that will drive us to our destination.

> *"If it were just about setting a direction we would be at
> our destination already. It's much more than this. It's
> about the daily practices that we must follow. This is what
> provides the fuel to keep our vehicles moving forward."*
> - Christopher Lawrence

---

[11] Statisticbrain.com,. 'New Years Resolution Statistics | Statistic Brain'. N.p., 2015. Web. 9 Aug. 2015.

In the next chapter we will discuss how we take our vision and turn it into a reality by establishing daily practices. Please remember, I recommend reading the entire chapter before doing the work.

End of Chapter Reflection

You don't know what you don't know, but now that you know what you know:

...What has now become more painful?
...Therefore, what is an action you have been avoiding that you now need to take?

...What has now become blatantly obvious?
...Therefore, what is an easy action that is right in front of you that you can take right now?

...What is going to become more rewarding now?
...Therefore, what is an action that you have always wanted to take that you just haven't gotten around to?

CHAPTER 6

KEEPING YOURSELF FUELED: ESTABLISHING DAILY PRACTICES

In addition to your compelling and inspiring vision, you must create daily practices that support the vision. This is how you close the gaps to get from your current state to your desired end state. These literally become the steps and answer the question "How do I get there?". The last chapter had 4 steps. I would like to continue these steps from our previous chapter to ensure you understand that this is a linear process.

The last step, Step 4, was to create a compelling and inspiring vision. This should be a simple statement that excites you and gives you direction. Now we have to take that vision and put it into practice by continuing with Step 5

5. Identify practices that you currently have that may be keeping you where you are. These could be things like:
   - Not telling my boss what is important to me
   - Waiting for my boss to schedule my reviews rather than taking the initiative to schedule them myself
   - Turning right to go home instead of turning left to go to the gym

These are the things that are keeping you exactly where you are today. If we don't acknowledge this then we will stay in the same place. This section requires your deepest introspection and honesty.

6. Identify practices that you need to develop in order to see your vision come to fruition. These could be things like:
    • Schedule my reviews for a year in advance with my boss
    • Track three tasks per day that put me in my peak state and three tasks per day that put me in my weak state.
    • Eat fresh leafy greens every meal without salad dressing before I eat anything else on my plate.

7. Determine metrics or criteria – How will you know that you are successfully on the way to achieving the results you would like to achieve?

By doing this you are making small shifts that will eventually have a long-term meaningful impact on your life and the results you experience.

For quick reference, I have provided the steps again in a summarized format:

1. Review your priorities from Chapter 2
2. Review your eulogy from Chapter 3
3. Determine which area in your life you would like to create a short-term vision
4. Create a compelling and inspiring vision
5. Determine what practices you currently have that keep you in your current state
6. Determine new practices you need to adopt immediately to create your future state and obtain your desired results
7. Determine metrics or criteria to know you are successfully on the way to achieving the results you'd like to see

Okay, we need to pause here for a minute because there are a few things that can go wrong and when that happens we can run out of fuel, pull over and get out of the vehicle, or in some extreme cases, crash our vehicle never to be driven again. I have seen this where clients choose a vision, fall in love with it, and then nearly work themselves to death trying to achieve it. In the cases where they don't achieve it they feel completely defeated and want to give up.

If this happens it can be because you may have created a vision that isn't suitable for your life at this time. This is only considered true if you have really tried and done the work to make it happen. Remember, hard work and correct action are required. If you have done these things then you might need to troubleshoot to see what may be preventing you from moving forward with your vision. Let's do that now so that you can be fully prepared for what may come. I am not saying that these things will happen, simply that they can happen.

Willingness & Ability Model

Sometimes we think we want something and then we see what is required to get there. Then we realize that what we wanted is no longer in line with our values and beliefs. An example of this could be perhaps, everyone wants to be an Olympic athlete, the truth is, most of us aren't willing to dedicate 16+ hours a day to training and being told when to eat, sleep, socialize, and relax. When we discover what is truly required we may no longer be interested.

This could also be seen with someone who thinks they want to be a business owner but then they see the amount of time and money required to get started and realize it may not be feasible for them because they are about to have triplets in the family. In this case the time and cost investment of being a business owner may not be in line with how they need or want to spend their time.

If you lose sight of your vision for any reason, there are two key questions that you must ask yourself.

The first one is, "What is my willingness to do this?"

The second one is, "What is my ability to do this?"

If you consider your ability – it is almost always high. As human beings we are incredibly adaptable to new situations. For example, we all have the ability to make a million dollars a year.

Ability is part of the combination we require for success. We can close the gaps on ability quite easily. Often though, ability has nothing to do with it. Instead, it may be that we do not have the willingness to do what it takes to make a million dollars a year.

Our ability to change is extremely high but our willingness tends to be a lot lower. Willingness is based on a few different things. As human beings, the only thing that makes you different from the guy who is making a million dollars a year right now is how you see the world and what you choose to be your priorities. There are plenty of average people who make tons of money in all kinds of businesses (it's not just about money, I am using this to illustrate an easy example). When ability is low, it is very easy to close the gap with training or education. When willingness is low we must take a completely different approach. Below are three models you may wish to try to increase your motivation and see your vision become a reality.

The Pain Versus Reward Model

1. The first thing that you might ask yourself is, "What is good about staying where I am today?" The answer will not be "nothing". There is some payoff to doing what you are doing today and staying where you are. You could shift this question and say, "What is so painful about changing that I would rather stay where I am today?"

2. To create more willingness and increase your motivation you might then ask, "What is so painful about my current

circumstance that I absolutely have to change?" Don't be afraid to be ridiculous. If we can exaggerate the pain of where you are today, the chances of increasing your willingness to make changes goes up significantly.

For example, maybe you want to entice yourself to negotiate a raise with your boss. You might remind yourself that if you don't ask for a raise you will never be able to go on an overseas vacation. You might also state that when the cost of living goes up you could be homeless and perhaps you'll never pay off that credit card. Or maybe you won't be able to purchase a home. Your kids will starve, etc.

3. Then finish this off by answering, "What are the awesome rewards of getting the results I desire?"

    For example, if I get that raise then I can start saving for that vacation and I'll feel totally secure with taking on a second mortgage, etc.

    In many cases, it could be in your best interests to increase your tolerance to risk. In other words, get more comfortable with being uncomfortable. In fact, if you experience no discomfort along this journey, you probably need to set your vision a little bit higher.

The Social Accountability Model

Another way to increase willingness is to use social accountability. This is where you tell a number of friends what you are up to and they check in with you to ensure you are keeping your word. My criteria for this is to use friends that are at arm's length – people that are a little bit further away than your best friend and your family. When we use our closest friends and family it can have two negative impacts. The first being, they sometimes tend to let us get away with things we don't want ourselves to get away with. The second being, it places additional expectations on someone who may already have a lot of responsibility in ensuring our success. This can lead to unnecessary conflict.

The idea is to choose someone who you trust and know well enough to make the ask, someone that might bring a little bit of humorous embarrassment if you didn't follow through with your vision, but not so much that you go to a place of shame and self-loathing. The very best way to approach this is to set some ground rules that you can follow. The conversation could be very cavalier. It could go something like this:

> *"Hi Elaine, we've known each other for a little while now. I have come to enjoy the time we spend together and I am wondering if we could try something together. Don't worry, I promise it's not weird! I am doing a little experiment with myself and I'm wondering if you would participate? Don't say 'yes' until you hear what I've got in mind. I am trying to hold myself accountable to changing my attitude at work. My goal is to make this job work out really well for me. I'm going to start by going in early every day to say hello to all of the staff rather than just coming in and going straight to my desk. I'd like to see what kind of impact this has on the workplace and my attitude towards it. I'm going to be tracking my progress daily. All I need from you is a weekly check-in over the phone for two to three minutes. This will make sure I'm staying on track. The best way you can help me is to ask one simple question and making one simple statement. The question is, 'How is the experiment coming?' And the statement is, 'Keep doing what you are doing, Chuck, I can see you making progress!' What do you think? You can say 'no' too and then we can talk about the weather! I promise I won't be offended!"*

You will want to be very careful with this one. As I mentioned, you don't want to create a situation where you create a parent-child relationship with this friend or where you invite someone into your vulnerability that has no business being there.

The Expect Failure Or Don't Define It Model

Finally, you must expect that failure is going to come at some point on your journey. Our vehicles breakdown, require maintenance, and sometimes, we need a new one. Failure is a blessing if you allow it to be. In fact, as a business owner and a human being I can tell you that the best things have come from my failures. Most business owners know that most of what they do will fail, they will get more "no's" than "yes's" in the beginning, and a lot of time and effort will go towards things that will never come to fruition or, when they do, they never work out the way they were planned. These are what allow us to grow! We must embrace these experiences. I know that for me in my business, I look forward to potential clients saying "no" to one of my offers because I need those "no's" to get to the "yes's". When I *want* to hear the "no" I get really brave and start to say and do things that feel a little fun and crazy. I feel more relaxed because I'm not banking on getting a new client so the pressure is off. Most often, this is when the clients say yes.

One other option is to not define what failure looks like. Instead you could look at every experience and the results to those experiences as a range of success. This is what I did in order to overcome my fear to start a business. I decided that even if my business had to close its doors it would be a massive success because I will have learned something and contributed to something that is so meaningful to me. By doing this there was no way I could fail.

Expect failure or choose not to define failure. Either way you win!
- Christopher Lawrence

Do you remember Holland that we spoke of earlier? Remember how I told you she had a few false starts on her journey. This could also be defined as a series of failures. As I mentioned, she decided she had to focus on fitness and cleaning her home as her first step because discovering her dream job seemed so far away at the time. At the time of writing this book, she has made significant progress in both of these areas and then, quite naturally found herself taking personal training classes to become a personal fitness trainer. Along this journey, she realized that one of the things that put her in her peak state was taking things she had learned from her own personal fitness trainer and showing it and explaining it to other people. If she hadn't had her failures she never would have come to this place of realization and strength.

End of Chapter Reflection

You don't know what you don't know but now that you know what you know:

...What has now become more painful?
...Therefore, what is an action you have been avoiding that you now need to take?

...What has now become blatantly obvious?
...Therefore, what is an easy action that is right in front of you that you can take right now?

...What is going to become more rewarding now?
...Therefore, what is an action that you have always wanted to take that you just haven't gotten around to?

CHAPTER 7

ADJUST TO MAKE IT STICK

This is the part of our trip where most people begin to fail. We *Stop* to take stock of exactly where we are and what supplies we have. Then we *Think* in order to provide ourselves with focus. In other words, we determine which things are most important that need to be addressed first. Then we start to *Move*, so our vehicle is in motion and we are cruising down the road heading in a direction with clarity.

When we are driving we make adjustments all the time. We will stop for fuel, make repairs, or adjust our direction if we need to, because we know that if we don't, we aren't going to get there. This perhaps, is an example that stays only with driving in our conscious minds. When it comes to goal-setting people tend to do this differently. Usually after we start moving we will gain momentum quickly and then we seem to run out of fuel.

Jason is a client just like this. He was in our monthly workshop and group coach program. In the beginning he would do his weekly check-ins and come to the call. He was even able to finish the work that was required to *Move* and initially gained very good momentum. Eventually he ran out of fuel and stopped doing the work and attending the monthly phone coaching. What happened?

Jason experienced what so many people experience after they get going, the brilliant feeling we get when starting on a new path eventually begins to fade. The honeymoon is now over and the real work has to begin. Just like when we are on a trip, we have to evaluate our progress and make adjustments. We need to answer the question "what makes it stick?" Not everything we do will work so we have to make adjustments along the way.

There are two things that usually happen in these circumstances. The first is that we set a direction and we start to run out of fuel because we have lost sight of our compelling and inspiring vision or we haven't created the necessary daily practices to keep it going. The second reason is because we don't see progress so we think it isn't meant to happen and so we start to give up. This is why it's good to have a community of people or a coach or another social responsibility to keep you moving forward. Why does this happen? Because, we are seeking fulfillment and we are best motivated by quick-wins and fast, applicable rewards. When we don't see them quickly enough we start to lose momentum and our purpose for taking action becomes less relevant. Occasionally, this means we don't recognize when we have had a success or have defined what finished looks like.

> *"If things aren't working try making one or two small adjustments to your daily practices before you blow up the whole system!"*
> - Christopher Lawrence

In order to overcome these challenges, we need to first evaluate our results then make correct adjustments. Ultimately, this will elevate our fulfillment. Correct adjustments usually require us to adjust (or change) one or two key daily practices at a time and give it time to take hold. If we change too much all at once we won't know what is working and what isn't. You have to think of this like planting seeds. They take time to grow and must be nurtured. I always think of the gym and healthy eating because so many people start out really well and they might get a month or two months in successfully (sometimes it's less than a week), but then they don't see results quickly enough so they decide to quit or, more often, the momentum slowly fades away. Change takes time. This chapter is all about creating significant results by establishing sustainability, which means we have to stay fluid while we apply conditioning–this only happens by doing the work.

Do you remember way back in Chapter 1 where I said that no matter where you are on your journey, you can move left or right at any time if you need to in the Dream Job Evolution Process Diagram? The whole process to get you results is wonderfully linear on paper, but at times you may be required to move left or right and up or down out of sync. That's real life, and that's wonderful... even if we can't see it as a blessing at the time.

Ironically, as I started to write this chapter about adjusting, which is really all about keeping the momentum going, I started to struggle with my own momentum. I started to feel writer's fatigue and wanted to stop to do something else. My brain was moving in all sorts of directions and couldn't seem to get focused. I had so much to say it overwhelmed me. I didn't want to miss anything. I wanted to call my friends and talk about how I was stuck and couldn't seem to move forward. What I did, and needed to do, was very quickly go back to *Think* and *Move* to revisit my vision and the things that filled me up. This pulled me forward and kept me going.

In this chapter, we are going to discuss some foolproof ways to *Adjust* your vehicle so you can keep your momentum going. Think of it as the oil change, which includes a 21-point inspection. After going so far and doing so much we need to *Stop*, *Think*, and *Move* again. Our emphasis will be on adjusting the work we have completed in the first three phases of the **Dream Job Discovery Process** diagram. Think of this chapter as a troubleshooting chapter. The general concept can be broken down into five steps, which will look very familiar to you because we have already analyzed steps 2, 3, and 4 in great detail. The idea behind this is not to go straight back to the beginning and make this a labour intensive, repetitive task but rather, on a weekly basis, physically look at your vision and your daily practices. It's a good idea to schedule this into your calendar to create the habit. I check mine every Wednesday morning. I schedule fifteen minutes for myself to complete this work but I can usually accomplish it in two minutes or less when things are going well. You will want to ask yourself a series of questions:

1. Am I on track and starting to see, feel or hear the results I want?
    a. If so, CONGRATULATIONS! Keep going, keep planting and watering seeds, and keep doing what you are doing! Check back next week. This is your personal benchmark
    b. If not, go to Step 2

2. ***Stop*** – What am I observing to be the facts in this situation?
    a. What am I actually doing and not doing?
    b. How do I feel about what I have just written?
    c. Is that perception getting in the way of my own success?

3. ***Think*** – What is important about this situation?
    a. What needs my focus at this time?
    b. Do I need to add clarity to my filters?
    c. Has anything changed or is there new information to consider?

4. ***Move*** – Is my vision clear, compelling, and inspiring?
    a. Am I following my daily practices?
    b. What needs to happen to make this work? (Instead of asking, "How do I do this?", shift your language to ask "What needs to happen to get it done?" because here we have implied that a solution is near and "how" tends to put us in the stuck place.)
    c. Is a shift in gear necessary to pull me forward to my vision or goal? If so, what is it? (If you don't know what it is then ask yourself, "what seems reasonable to try?". Don't give yourself an easy way out of this question. Remove "I don't know" from your vocabulary.

5. Make tweaks in your daily practices _only_ if necessary. Don't quit so easily. Trust the process and keep going!

You might be interested to know that I did reach out to Jason and got him back on the monthly calls. I asked him to stick around for one more month and if we couldn't resolve his concerns, I would recommend another coach for him. After reviewing, it turns out Jason was adjusting all along. The problem was that he was adjusting because he was bored and the results were taking longer than he wanted. So, to keep his mind busy and growing, he would make adjustments every single week. None of the seeds he planted were nurtured long enough to see any growth.

We can be a society of impatience. We get everything we need instantly because truly, it's possible. Sometimes we want to **Adjust** because we are bored. We look to meet our need for variety and growth when we do this. Sometimes we need to tweak quickly because of unforeseen circumstances; however, we should not adjust just because we are bored. We adjust because we have a need to adjust to get a desired end result. Then, when we do it, it needs to be in a correct way that truly aligns our practices to our ultimate desired end-state. Do not look at modifying anything as a knee-jerk reaction. You have to know exactly why you are doing it! Sometimes the only adjustment we need is in our perspective.

Jason had to go back and **Stop** to re-evaluate what was really happening. In the end, we came up with a different way to stimulate him. What we decided to do was create a game out of his daily practices. We did something slightly different every day, created a points system (because he was motivated this way), and a little friendly competition with some of the others on the call. This worked well and he started to see some significant results.

Jason is not alone here. Every single human being on Earth has felt discouragement around some goal or initiative they were trying to achieve that wasn't coming to fruition. These moments are going to come but they will also go. To help you better navigate through these bumps on the road, I have identified some possible challenges that can arise while we are on this journey as well as some suggested solutions to overcome those challenges.

Boredom

In this scenario you are feeling bored about your daily practices and your vision. There could be a number of reasons for this. One reason is that your vision might not be compelling and inspiring enough for you, which means it might need some tweaks. If you don't have good reasons for doing it, you surely won't be inspired to do it. Ensure your vision is inspiring and make sure that your daily practices feel unique and fun to you. Ensure they put you in your peak state.

Lost Momentum

This is when you thought you were onto something really amazing and exciting but now that a few weeks have passed you aren't so excited about it anymore. In this case we can look at something like your eulogy and remember the ways in which we know we must spend our lives to ensure they are meaningful to us. We might also go back and take a look at your Peak State Tasks and see what fills you up. Finding a way to integrate these into the Daily Practices can become very important. Here you must get creative! This could be as simple as creating a "Peak State Playlist" on your mobile device. Listening to a few minutes of pumped up music while visualizing your desired end result is sometimes just enough to keep us rolling through the daily practices. In fact, listening to this playlist could be one of your daily practices.

Feeling Discouraged

This usually happens when people have had a series of failures in a row and they aren't seeing any results. It is in these moments when we have to persevere. We must reach deep into our souls and realize this is happening for a reason. Here, imagine you are like a pioneer. You are the first person to a new land. There are no houses, streets, or cars. In fact, food is scarce too because you have to hunt and scavenge for it. This is what setting and achieving a goal can be like. While many people may have accomplished what you would like to accomplish, it may be new territory for you. If we perceive ourselves as pioneers, then we have no choice but to survive and make our circumstances work. If we don't then we face the possibility of dying. This may sound extreme but, like most life on Earth, if it is not growing and thriving, then it is usually dying either literally or metaphorically. Do whatever it takes (that is healthy) to change your state of mind to break through the discouragement!

Fear

What happens when you realize that one of the daily practices on your journey is going to force you to face one of your greatest fears? Feel the fear and do it anyway! I realize this sounds simple in concept but harder in practice. I am going to use a personal example here to illustrate my point.

My job requires me to travel but I was afraid to fly! In fact, I was so afraid to fly that I didn't fly for three solid years. This really interrupted how I wanted to live my life and it was not in line with my eulogy. When we start to approach our fears, we tend to try and rationalize them away. I did this too. I thought about flying for three years. I thought about how I could overcome the fear. I tried to rationalize the fear away too. I know all the stats about flying and how safe it truly is and I still couldn't get on a plane. The truth is, you cannot rationalize away a fear. This is partially what makes it a fear – the fact that it is irrational. I knew that the only way to deal with this was going to be getting on a plane. I booked my first flight in three years and stressed for three weeks while I waited for the flight to take off. I worked with a psychologist on some tools to help me deal with the panic I knew was coming.

It took me some time but eventually what I was able to do was compartmentalize the fear so that I only experienced it during takeoff. In fact, the part that most people hate is turbulence and landing. For me, those have become my favourite parts of the flight. To help lock in these new feelings I decided to get on a small two-seater plane and take a flying lesson. During this lesson I actually had the opportunity to fly the plane without the instructors help for a period of time. You can bet I was sweating bullets. In fact, it's a lot like the first time you get behind the wheel of the car. It can be a very nerve wracking experience. I continue to expose myself to flying. Without this I would not have been able to move forward with my vision for my life and my overall fulfillment would never have been met.

One of the very best ways to deal with fear is through mindfulness. We are going to speak more on this in the next chapter but if you have not yet explored an 8-week Mindfulness Based Stress Reduction (MBSR) course I highly recommend it! There are plenty of free classes on the Internet. If you reach out to me I'll share with you my favourite one.

> *"The best way to deal with fear is through mindfulness!"*
> - Christopher Lawrence

Too Comfortable to Change

You will experience this if the pain of changing is greater than the comfort you currently experience in your life right now. I spent over a decade in the field of corporate change management. The very best way to resolve this problem is by increasing your perceived pain of where you are now so that it is so completely unbearable that you have no choice but to change. Write down this pain so that you can remember it and remind yourself of it often. Also remember to write down the rewards of making the change. Make them big and wonderful. This gives you reason to change.

Confusion: Keep Losing Clarity or Focus

This happens when we are not hearing our own voice anymore or we have conflicting values and beliefs. I recommend revisiting the **Dream Job Discovery Process** diagram from the beginning of this book in a detailed way. If this is inherent in your life, it is likely time for a new perspective and some accountability. I strongly recommend that you consider working with a coach who is versed in motivating people to take imperfect, inspired action.

Expectations Not Being Met

This is where, eventually, everyone gets stuck and it's like quicksand. Here we have two situations that arise. The first is that we have set unrealistic expectations on ourselves for what we are able to accomplish. The second is that we perceive or know that others have placed expectations upon us that are in conflict with what we are trying to achieve. I see this a lot with clients at all levels of the career and life coaching I provide. Realistically it can take anywhere from 3 to 36 months to really lock onto a clear career path. The average is usually around 6 to 12 months. And even after we do this we must spend our time overcoming all of the obstacles that get in the way of achieving the career the client desires. We have to set our expectations very clearly and allow them to change when they cannot be met. Expectations must remain fluid.

On the flip side, we may end up in a situation where the people in our inner circle do not support, agree, care, or like the changes we are trying to implement in our careers and lives. Usually this is because they perceive it will affect them or their relationship with you in some negative way.

Whether you are placing expectations on yourself or you perceive or know that others are placing them on you, you might consider doing an "in my control" versus "out of my control" exercise.

Control Exercise

In this exercise, you take a piece of paper and draw a line down the centre of the page. At the top, write the current situation you are faced with. Label one column "These are the things that are in my control in this situation" and label the other column "These are the things that are out of my control in this situation". Start to list everything that is in and out of your control. When you have completed this activity cut the paper in half on the line you drew, cross out and throw away everything that is on the "out of my control" side because you no longer have permission to focus on what is out of your control. If these things are truly out of your control there is no point in putting any more focus on them. Then give yourself permission to focus _only_ on the things that fall on the "in my control" side of the paper. If you focus on what is in your control you will adjust your expectations to align with what your current reality is, thus allowing you to feel empowered to continue to move forward.

Sometimes, this does mean that we can lose friends in the process. I am a big fan of keeping relationships where they can be kept. Even the most difficult relationships can be so incredibly rewarding. There can come a time where these relationships do not serve our best interests any longer; they become an obstacle to us achieving our dreams and reaching career success. The mindset we had when we found these friends might not be the mindset that we are trying to create now and when those around us can't seem to understand, sometimes we lose these relationships. This is not about going through your list of contacts and crossing off the people who you don't think will get it. What this is about is giving yourself permission to hear your own voice while being patient with those around you, because they might not yet understand the transition you are going through.

I am reminded of people who have overcome addiction in their lives. When people go from being completely high or drunk or addicted to anything, to being sober and stable and not addicted, they do change as people. They are different. In this process they may lose friends along the way and it might not even be their enablers, sometimes it is those around them that don't understand why they don't talk, look, or behave in the same way. Anyone moving to a behavior that serves their best interest (like sobriety) cannot be the same person they were when they became an addict.

You might experience this too and I strongly encourage you to be patient with yourself and those around you. Remember, they don't know what you are thinking, or how you are feeling, and they likely don't see the world the same way you do and never will because they have their own unique set of motivations, beliefs, and values. With patience and a strategic approach almost any relationship can be salvaged if you choose it to be, whether it is intimate or platonic.

I believe that this is similar to any significant change we create in our lives. For example, look at those who have a self-proclaimed, mid-life crisis. A stereotypical view of this is that a (usually) white, heterosexual male buys a new sports car, starts dressing differently, and then works out like a mad man in an effort to reclaim his youth. What I see is a person who is in so much pain living the daily grind, so miserable, because he invested in a truth that doesn't represent who he is as a person today. For him to become happy again he cannot be the same person that he was before. His expectations have not been fluid to adapt to a change that could be occurring internally or externally in his environment. There are many ways to resolve this, although I question the search for authentic happiness in material items or vanity. Usually these things prove to be less authentic; however, what this can do is reignite the spark that has been buried or missing for so many years. And the people in his life may not be able to understand this right away.

~~~

How can I make this all relate to my career?

This is a very good question. You might feel, at this point, we have strayed away from discovering your dream job or evolving your current job into your dream job. This is not the case. Remember I mentioned that this was about your whole life as much as it is about your career. I would like to make a direct tie back to challenges people have in the workplace to ensure the concepts are locking in. Below are a few scenarios that you may experience at work that slow you down from achieving your vision. I have provided some tips and tricks to get you thinking about ways of approaching your unique situation and to ultimately get you moving again.

Feeling Unfulfilled at Work

Look at what you are doing on a day-to-day basis. Are 80% of your tasks putting you in a peak state or in line with your personal vision? If not, it's time to make some adjustments.

Bad Boss / Bad Coworker

Most of this is about communication. Most leaders are not properly trained and if you say nothing, they know nothing and won't be able to help you. The same applies to your coworkers. Most interoffice conflicts that I have seen come from passive behavior – when people are too scared to have a face-to-face conversation about what is bothering them. When you have a bad boss or coworker, you require a strategy. Do not simply say what's on your mind in that moment and expect amazing results. Instead go through the same process we took ourselves through.

> *Stop* – What are the facts in this situation?
> *Think* – What is really important here?
> *Move* – What needs to happen to get this resolved?
> *Adjust* – Keep the conversation open. Did it work? If not, tweak.

Living Pay-Cheque to Pay-Cheque

You have three options and they are simple. You will have to excuse my blunt approach, but I have seen clients, friends, peers and family members fixate on this topic of "not paid enough" for far too long. I get it! Many of us will never feel like we are paid enough for the work we do, so consider the following:

Option 1 – Ask for a raise

You can increase your chances of doing this if you learn what is of value to your boss and company and provide that value to them, then learn to influence and negotiate. You will also need to know what the company's compensation structure is if they have one and are willing to share it. Be prepared to build your case and know that most often we are paid what is in the budget and not what we are worth or deserve.

Option 2 – Find a job that pays more

Be careful here. You might make more but you might be miserable when you find out that what you have to do operates 80% or more in your Weak State Tasks. Sometimes the grass isn't greener on the other side of the fence but that doesn't mean you can't continue to work on watering the grass no matter where you land.

Option 3 – Change your blueprint around money

Learn to think of money in a different way completely. You can do this in such a way where spending or donating money becomes so valuable to you that you don't care what you have to do to make more. You can also do this by realizing that all sorts of people can make a healthy living with savings on a very tight budget. A client at one of my events was born and raised in Eastern Europe. His blueprint on money was very different from what we usually see here in North America. He was supporting his stay-at-home wife and two kids on a budget of less than $50,000 in the third most expensive city in Canada. He claimed that he was "abundant" and that he didn't feel the need to make an expression of himself through material things. This is almost unheard of for that amount of money supporting a family in North America, but it is possible!

Should I Quit My Job?

I can't answer that for you but I can give you some guidelines. Start by asking, "am I able to influence and negotiate in this job?". No job will ever be perfect, especially if you decide to own your own business (although it is incredibly rewarding). You must take stock. If you can influence and negotiate, put your focus on getting at least 80% of your tasks to be ones that put you in your Peak State. Also know there are fluctuations in this and we will all have periods below 80%. It's the extended periods that can make us experience feelings of depression, anxiety, or dissatisfaction. When this happens for long periods is when you might consider quitting. You could also ask yourself, "Can I afford to quit right now?" This last question is a funny one, because sometimes we can't financially afford to quit but mentally and emotionally we need to. I have seen clients quit, get fired, or laid off and have it be the best kind of freedom and motivation they had ever experienced in their life! Be careful with this one.

I Can't Leave My Terrible Job, How Do I Make This My Dream Job?

If you are truly in a position where you cannot leave your job and you see no way out of it whatsoever then you must focus on your vision and your blueprint. If your blueprint is set to being an Olympic athlete and you have never worked out a day in your life and now you are 35 years old... it is unlikely that you will succeed, not impossible, but unlikely. You need to change the beliefs and values you have. You need to manage your expectations and focus only on what is in your control. There are people who have done this, like Prisoners of War or Holocaust survivors. You also see this in examples of Sanitary Engineers (garbage men and women) and some of them love their jobs. People who have children and feel they have to work at a job they despise because they want their kids to go to post-secondary school may have also adopted this thinking.

To make your existing job your dream job, you will have to change how you approach your job completely. You might have to adjust your expectations to expect very little in return but give a lot. You may have to come into the worst place in the world with a smile on your face and say "hello" to everybody first thing in the morning. Whatever you do, don't give up and don't go to that hardened, bitter place. It's never too late. Reach out for help if you need it.

End of Chapter Reflection

You don't know what you don't know, but now that you know what you know:

...What has now become more painful?

...Therefore, what is an action you have been <u>avoiding</u> that you now need to take?

...What has now become blatantly obvious?

...Therefore, what is an <u>easy</u> action that is right in front of you that you can take right now?

...What is going to become more rewarding now?

...Therefore, what is an action that you have <u>always wanted to take</u> that you just haven't gotten around to?

CHAPTER 8

BE IN YOUR WHOLE-LIFE EXPERIENCE: A CASE FOR MINDFULNESS

Congratulations! Now that you have made it to this portion of the book you are on the home stretch. By this point, you have done the work and you have something incredible to be proud about.

Now that you have learned to **Adjust** your vehicle you will be able to drive to your destinations with confidence. In time, this will become a subconscious activity where, with practice, you will know exactly how to **Stop**, **Think**, **Move,** and **Adjust** your vehicle without even knowing you are doing it. It's going to become very natural, just like driving. When actual driving becomes a part of our subconscious mind, we can start to enjoy the scenery and the driving itself rather than worrying about all of the little things that might come up along the way. We can just **Be** with the driving.

You see, humans are curious creatures, and to be honest they don't like to stay in one place for too long. I suspect when many of you achieve your first vision you will say, "What now?" It is important that we answer this question because if we don't, it can sabotage what we have created in order to feel significant and create variety.

When you learn to just *Be,* this is when you are most able to have a whole-life experience. A meaningful whole-life experience is about having an experience or series of experiences where we are able to sustain our judgment for a period of time and see the blessing in all of it rather than rushing to any conclusions. What this means is that we have to be grateful and celebrate every aspect of our journey. This is what ultimately locks in those good feelings that make us want to keep growing and trying.

We can also refer to this as our flow state. This is the state where you are performing in your life fully immersed, inspired, and energized. The state where things just seem to flow and you experience full enjoyment and involvement in the process of living. The more time we spend practicing, creating, and achieving our visions the more time we spend in our flow state

Sheri first came to me for her job. She didn't want to leave but wanted to shift her blueprint so that she could feel vibrancy around it again as she moved her way towards retirement. She couldn't seem to find her flow state but she didn't stop trying. She kept going through the five-step process. After reviewing *Stop* a few times, we noticed one little nugget that we decided to explore more. This was in regards to her environment. She gave herself a medium to high rating in that area. But I decided to ask her about it anyway. She commented that her office was overflowing with papers that she had printed from the internet that she wanted to read, filled with unfiled documents that needed to be put away, and a huge binder full of to-do lists. At first glance, when we looked at her eulogy and her vision, the office and lists seemed so inconsequential. Upon further probing though, it became clear that the state of her office was what was getting in the way. It was a reflection of what was happening on the inside of Sheri. The lists that needed to be sorted, filed, completed, or recycled were a metaphor for her entire life – it was all unfinished business.

I could see the office was killing her flow state. It had been in this state for a number of years. She said that she was going to get to it in the coming weeks. This wasn't good enough for me. I asked her when exactly she was going to do it. She looked at me funny and kind of frowned, "Saturday?". Then I asked her which stack of papers she was going to start sorting first and she said, "The stack closest to the door" and she smiled. She said, "It's getting real then, isn't it?". We both laughed. We slowly came up with a solid plan of action. Her vision had changed and her rituals had changed. Her new vision was to *finally clean the office NOW so that she could get back to enjoying her life and supporting her husband and kids!* She changed her daily practice. It was all going to be completed over two days. She immediately implemented the following daily practices until the office was completely sorted:

- She communicated to the family that this was her number one priority and she must be left alone until the job was completed. She did not need any additional interruptions to her flow state at this time.
- She planned exactly when she would clean and when she would take her breaks.
- She came up with a policy to only spend a maximum of 20 seconds on any given sheet of paper and then she would have to make a decision about what to do with that paper.
- She would be finished cleaning it in one week (by the next time she met with me).
- If she got stuck or wasn't going to get it done she had to call me so we could discuss another plan of attack.

By the time she left my office she had hit her flow state. She was feeling so motivated and ready and willing to take action. She worked the entire weekend and one entire evening after work before it was all completed. It was incredible! Not only was the office incredible, but so was the transformation in her. She created a whole-life experience. She came back with joy in her heart, tears in her eyes, and laughter in her belly. She could finally move forward. Sheri was finally free to experience the rest of her life.

The work couldn't stop though. We had to answer the question "What now?" because the chance of Sheri falling back into a messy office was great if we didn't change her complete perception about it. She had to now have the mind of a person who has a clean office. We focused on creating a new set of daily practices, we adjusted her eulogy to include this story, and we provided her with a fresh short-haul destination – remember, this helps us to create the kind of vision that provides a quick short-term reward.

I ran into Sheri recently, almost a year since that time. She told me that her office was still clean and the real celebration comes from seeing it clean every day. She still feels free and tells people about this story. It was never about Sheri's office. It was about the burden she placed on herself about what the office represented, years of unfinished business. While cleaning the office she did not complete the unfinished business, instead she cleared her mind and opened herself up for a truly amazing life.

This is what I mean by having a whole-life experience.

In order to do this, we must never fall asleep at the wheel. Sometimes we are going to though. But you will know when this happens because you are going to start to experience disillusionment and non-fulfillment again. When this happens you will need to go back and **Stop**. This is why the Dream Job Evolution Process diagram has a big arrow pointing back to the **Stop** box with a note that says "Go back to 'Stop' if non-fulfillment is experienced for *prolonged* periods!"

I usually see a couple of specific things that can impact your ability to enjoy the **Be** stage successfully. The first is that people go back to **Stop** because they don't know how to stand in their own greatness, so they manifest problems in order to keep climbing out of the hole. This in itself has a payoff. The second is that people aren't aware that they have fallen out of their flow state until months or years of damage have been done. Usually when this happens self-loathing and guilt come with it.

To counteract this, I *strongly* recommend adopting a nearly daily mindfulness practice – which in this case could include meditation. I do this personally and my clients that do it agree that it has significantly impacted their lives in a positive way. The science behind mindfulness meditation is solid and it brings about an acute kind of awareness. Think about yourself as having the acute self-awareness of a Jedi Knight where you know when the Dark Side is looming over you and about to strike!

Mindfulness is essentially a very specific form of meditation where an individual focuses on their five senses by paying attention to their breath, thoughts, body sensations (including pain), thoughts, sounds, sights, and tastes. While it is Eastern in its origin, it does not require any spiritual beliefs or practices. This is not about spirituality (although one can have a seemingly spiritual experience). This is not about guiding oneself through a path of trees in a forest. Mindfulness is about paying attention in a particular way without expectation, judgment, or labels.

To name just a few of the incredible benefits it has, mindfulness supports people with chronic pain, anxiety, depression, a busy mind, overeating, anger, frustration, sadness, fear, grief, acceptance, mental and physical health, concentration, judgment, expectations, obsessive compulsive disorder, stress, heart disease, high blood pressure, sleep, interpersonal conflicts, and substance abuse.

Mindfulness is not a cure, it is not a miracle, and it is not a woo-woo religious practice. Mindfulness has been studied extensively by a number of scientists throughout history including John Kabat-Zinn, PhD. He took the very best of mindfulness practice and turned it into an 8 week program called Mindfulness Based Stress Reduction or MBSR.

With this said, you must go into a mindfulness practice with the mindset of expecting nothing at all to occur. It sounds so counter-intuitive to take more of our day and fill it with another activity and initially expect no reward out of it at all. I get it! I did a self-paced, 8-week MBSR program at home that I found for free on the Internet. It required six days of 30-minute meditations for eight weeks and one day of study, which took between 45 minutes to an hour.

> *"When practicing mindfulness, expect nothing at all. This is how you will achieve the best results!"*
> - Christopher Lawrence

Initially I was very frustrated. Sitting still for 30 minutes doing nothing but paying attention to my breath was not my idea of a good time and seemed very unfulfilling and counter-intuitive when I had so much work to do. Then I learned that what I was *practicing* was "frustration" and I wasn't in fact practicing mindfulness at all. So I learned to become curious. Isn't it a curious thing that sitting still for 30 minutes and doing nothing at all (something I'm sure I used to beg for when I worked in corporate) was so frustrating? I mean, really think about this. Isn't it a curious and funny thing that sitting still for 30 minutes can be so frustrating and anxiety-causing for some people? I still laugh about it now, just like I did then.

I have seen clients who have adopted a practice of mindfulness move from being in complete pain and suffering mentally, physically, and emotionally, to experiencing joy and happiness. Sometimes the pain and suffering went away but this does not mean that the pain and suffering goes away for everybody. What does happen though, is people learn to have a different relationship with pain where they perceive it in such a way that the experience of suffering simply becomes an experience rather than something we must fight or overcome. In some cases these experiences even become joyful.

Without mindfulness it is impossible to even recognize a Whole-Life Experience, let alone enjoy it. Ultimately this is what will put you in a true state of **Being**.

The Power of Celebration and Gratitude

We mentioned the importance of celebration in Chapter 5 when we were talking about celebrating to lock in the feelings of a job well done or to lock in a new habit. I cannot emphasize this point enough. Celebration is extremely powerful. Similarly, gratitude is fundamental to extreme success and a happy life. The following quote was found on Deepak Chopra's *Chopra Centered Lifestyle* blog page. It illustrates the importance of gratitude far better than I ever could.

> *Many scientific studies, including research by renowned psychologists Robert Emmons and Michael McCullough, have found that people who consciously focus on gratitude experience greater emotional wellbeing and*

physical health than those who don't. In comparison with control groups, those who cultivated a grateful outlook:

- *Felt better about their lives as a whole*
- *Experienced greater levels of joy and happiness*
- *Felt optimistic about the future*
- *Got sick less often*
- *Exercised more regularly*
- *Had more energy, enthusiasm, determination, and focus*
- *Made greater progress toward achieving important personal goals*
- *Slept better and awoke feeling refreshed*
- *Felt stronger during trying times*
- *Enjoyed closer family ties*
- *Were more likely to help others and offer emotional support*
- *Experienced fewer symptoms of stress*

If you want more happiness, joy, and energy, gratitude is clearly a crucial quality to cultivate. It is a fullness of heart that moves us from limitation and fear to expansion and love. When we're appreciating something, our ego moves out of the way and we connect with our soul. Gratitude brings our attention into the present, which is the only place where miracles can unfold. The deeper our appreciation, the more we see with the eyes of the soul and the more our life flows in harmony with the creative power of the universe.[12]

Gratitude and celebration are extremely important to your success. I encourage you to learn more about gratitude and success so you fully understand the impact it can have on helping you have a Whole-Life Experience.

---

[12] Chopra, D. (n.d.). Cultivate the Healing Power of Gratitude. Retrieved November 15, 2015, from http://www.chopra.com/ccl/cultivate-the-healing-power-of-gratitude

End of Chapter Reflection

Careful, this one is different!

You don't know what you don't know, but now that you know what you know:

> ...What are you grateful for?

> ...What are you celebrating?

FINAL THOUGHTS

When To Ask For Help

We started our journey together by asking the question, "What is fulfillment?" And we answered this with a quote by best-selling author Denis E. Waitley, "It is not in the pursuit of happiness that we find fulfillment, it is in the happiness of pursuit". Achieving this is significant and can be difficult, particularly if you have spent most of your life (and most of us have) in the pursuit of happiness.

I have already mentioned how, unlike Waitley's statement, I didn't enjoy the journey in getting to the destination. And after over ten years in corporate Calgary, I was ready to leave because I was sick and tired, I was 35 pounds overweight, and experiencing depression. I found myself ruminating – recycling thoughts over and over again trying to solve the problem. I had finally settled on the fact that some people were just never meant to be happy doing certain types of work and that I was one of them. It wasn't until I went on a journey of self-exploration that has lasted, now for more than a decade, that I was able to enjoy the journey.

> *"It's not just about your job, it's about your life!*
> *So approach this work for your job, but change for your life"*
> - Christopher Lawrence

What I have tried to do is summarize the very best information, tools, and examples to help you look at your life holistically in order to discover your dream job. If you still feel stuck or are continually unfulfilled, it's time to reach out to someone. You are welcome to call or email us at Change My Life Coaching (www.ChangeMyLifeCoaching.ca).Our mission is to provide career coaching that leads to a more fulfilled life. We do this by providing uniquely customized, whole-life coaching programs that get results for unfulfilled working persons.

If you need or want to take your journey to the next level or if you need clarity on something in this book, don't wait! Reach out to me. This is what I do at Change My Life Coaching and I want you to love your job as much as I love mine

On that note, please allow me to wish you best wishes for life! I hope you reach out and tell me about your journey.

Many blessings.

REFERENCES

Buckingham, M., & Clifton, D. (2001). *Now, discover your strengths.* New York: Free Press.

Chopra, D. (n.d.). Cultivate the Healing Power of Gratitude. Retrieved November 15, 2015, from http://www.chopra.com/ccl/cultivate-the-healing-power-of-gratitude

Evans, Lisa. 'Global Employment: What Is The World Employment Rate?'. *The Guardian.* N.p., 2011. Web. 9 Aug. 2015.

Evans, Lisa. 'Global Employment: What Is The World Employment Rate?'. *the Guardian.* N.p., 2011. Web. 9 Aug. 2015.

Leo Tolstoy quote. (n.d.). Retrieved November 15, 2015, from http://www.brainyquote.com/quotes/quotes/l/leotolstoy105644.html

Marcus Buckingham quote. (n.d.). Retrieved November 15, 2015, from http://www.brainyquote.com/quotes/quotes/m/marcusbuck526901.html

Robbins, A. (1991). *Awaken the giant within: How to take immediate control of your mental, emotional, physical & financial destiny.* New York, N.Y.: Summit Books.

Robbins, A. Blog,. 'The 6 Human Needs: Why We Do What We Do -
Tony Robbins Blog'. N.p., 2013. Web. 9 Aug. 2015.

Statisticbrain.com,. 'New Years Resolution Statistics | Statistic Brain'.
N.p., 2015. Web. 9 Aug. 2015.

Vaynerchuk, Gary. *Crush It!*. [New York]: HarperStudio, 2009. Print.

ABOUT CHANGE MY LIFE COACHING

Established in 2012, Change My Life Coaching is a wellness business that provides a holistic approach to improving your life, career, or business through coaching. Clients learn to hear their own true voice and filter out the noise that often comes with belief systems. This noise can act as an obstacle to clients achieving their best life.

Clients discover and identify their true passions and destroy distortions in their thinking that get in the way of attaining their dreams. We help clients overcome mental, emotional, physical, and spiritual obstacles that may keep them from being successful. Clients sometimes realize that change is the only constant so learning to transition through change is key.

Change My Life Coaching is a team of professionals who provide practical and inspiring whole-life coaching solutions that positively impact every aspect of our client's lives, careers, and businesses. My personal mission at Change My Life Coaching is to provide life coaching that leads to a more fulfilled life. I do this by providing uniquely customized whole-life coaching programs that get results for unfulfilled working professionals, among others.

Change My Life Coaching will be the leading whole-life coaching organization across Canada with every coaching program customized to the unique needs and desires of our clients. My personal vision is to be the coach that best recognizes and conquers the challenges, stresses and worries of the working professional, among others, so you can embrace your passion and experience your best life.

ABOUT THE AUTHOR

Author Photo Credit: Randy Murray-Donohoe

Christopher Lawrence, Career and Life Coach, spent 10+ years working in the corporate world with a plethora of industries and companies. His focus was primarily in planning, strategy, and leadership of change management and communication where he worked with the five generations now in the work force. Christopher is now an author, passionate public speaker, trainer, facilitator and Certified Master Coach Practitioner (CMCP) who truly cares about the success of each and every single person he comes into contact with.

After spending 10 years as an active alumnus, 5 years as Chairperson of an academic advisory committee at the Southern Alberta Institute of Technology (SAIT) and 5 years as president of a Condominium Corporation, Christopher developed a huge passion for not only formal education but also experiential learning – education that comes from living life. Through this experience Christopher is able to identify and leverage personal experiences into something solid and tangible that can be used to help clients along their journey through life including career fulfillment.

Christopher has overcome adversity at every turn in his life. From being a high school drop out and recovered drug addict to successfully dealing with anxiety and depression. Christopher has learned to hear his own voice and now teaches his clients to do the same. Having personally dealt with body image issues, weight issues, hampering physical illness, and spiritual struggles – which ultimately led him down the path of attaining his Reiki Master and Reiki Teacher qualification — Christopher is able to help his clients see through the fog and gain clarity, and as Tony Robbins claims, "clarity is power"!

Leveraging these experiences, Christopher is able to draw you, the client, out of your head and into a space that allows you to connect to the inner dialogue, correct the distortions in your thinking, and help you to hear the inner you that already knows how to achieve your best life.

All of these things tie up into a nice package that looks at your whole life by starting at the core of who you are to ensure that all of the pieces are working together. Because of his practical experiences, Christopher is able to support individuals as they transition into new and wonderful (sometimes scary and risky) changes in their lives.

Christopher is a Certified Coach Practitioner, Certified Master Coach Practitioner, and Certified Rapid Results Coach.

Printed in the United States
By Bookmasters